EXIT THE GOOD WIFE

LOTUS CHEONG

PLATYPUS PUBLISHING

To my spirit guides Dr. Carole Setser and Sally McDonald, two amazing mothers who taught me rich life lessons and who left this earth early because they have accomplished their life contracts.

CONTENTS

PART 1
THE LIFE I WAS TOLD TO WANT

1

THE ANNIVERSARY THAT BROKE ME

"Ruin is a gift. Ruin is the road to transformation."
—Elizabeth Gilbert

Ugh. That smell. That awful, sour beer breath hits me like a slap across the face. I swear, it's not even just a smell anymore. It's a trigger. A warning. A flag raised high over the battlefield of my kitchen, declaring war on whatever tiny strand of patience I have left.

In that moment, standing there, looking at the man I married a lifetime ago, I want nothing more than to walk out. No, run out. Not just out of the room. Out of the house. Hell, out of this whole life.

Is it okay to feel like this?

Is it okay for a mom, yes, a mom, to want to pack up her clothes, grab her keys, and disappear because the very people she loves most are the ones making her feel completely, utterly repulsed?

Calm down.

Breathe.

Calm the f*** down.

You're a grown-ass woman. You can do this.

You don't have to love him right now. You don't even have to like him.

But you absolutely cannot lose your shit in front of the kids.

So what do you do?

You take a break. You walk out. Not forever, just long enough to keep your sanity intact. Say you're going rockhounding. Say you're going to find mushrooms. Say whatever you need to say that will let you breathe in silence for a few sacred hours. The truth is, you're not looking for rocks. You're looking for pieces of yourself that got buried under years of compromise and unmet expectations.

Twenty-five years.

Twenty-five years I've been married to this man. That's more than half my life. What did he do for our silver anniversary?

Nothing.

Absolutely nothing.

Not a card. Not a flower. Not even a "Hey, thanks for sticking with me through everything."

I sat on the couch while my best friend in Melbourne sent me pictures of her husband's celebration for their twenty-fifth. The whole yard was decked out. Lights, flowers, twinkling fairy dusts. It looked like Shakespeare threw up romance all over her lawn. He pampered her like she was royalty.

Me?

I got a "Where do you want to eat?"

That's it.

Check. Another year survived.

The thing is, I knew I didn't deserve much better. We've been circling the drain for months. Snapping. Silent. Avoiding. We don't touch. We don't laugh. We don't even argue properly anymore. We just sit in this weird emotional cold war, firing eye-rolls and passive-aggressive "I'm fine"s back and forth.

I've stopped showing affection because he stopped.

He stopped helping, caring, and seeing me. So I did too.

It seemed to be an endless circle of uncaring, each of us waiting for the other to blink first.

I asked him to retire. I practically begged. I thought, "Finally, we'll have time together. We'll slow down, reconnect, maybe even find our rhythm again." But what I really did was pull him out of the only identity he ever knew and handed him a version of life he didn't recognize. Or want.

Now he resents me.

I know it.

I can feel it in the way he sighs. The way he walks out of rooms when I walk in. The way he avoids eye contact during dinner. He's pissed that I asked him to trade his structured, predictable world for the chaos of family life. Now he feels useless. Like some outdated piece of furniture that's just taking up space.

He's not wrong.

I do expect him to step up. Cook. Help with chores. Be involved with the kids. I mean, why shouldn't he? I've been doing this for over two decades.

He asked me once, "So what are you gonna do now?"

And I snapped, "I'm going to keep working like I've always done. Raising kids, running the house, managing the invisible load. Just like I've always done. Alone."

Yeah. That didn't go over well.

Now we're here. Two tired, disappointed people orbiting the same house like strangers with shared responsibilities.

How did we get here?

How do two people who once laughed until their sides hurt now barely look each other in the eyes?

We're still married. But we're not okay.

And that realization is terrifying.

So pull up a chair, friend. Sip your cappuccino. Mine's dry, skinny, with a splash of stevia if you're wondering. And let me tell you the rest of this story.

Because it's not over.

If you're where I am right now, struggling, hurting, clinging, then maybe, just maybe, this next part will help you figure out where you want to go from here.

2

PRETTY, POLISHED, AND POWERLESS

"We teach girls to shrink themselves, to make themselves smaller. We say to girls, 'You can have ambition, but not too much.'"
 -*Chimamanda Ngozi Adichie*

I'm a spiritual person. I meditate. I don't subscribe to any specific religion, but I do believe this life is guided by something larger than ourselves. I've witnessed this whenever I experience pivotal struggles on my journey.

My journey started in Singapore, where I grew up in the seventies. It was a place still muddy, chaotic, and trying to find its footing after British rule. Floods were normal. There were dirt roads and street hawkers yelling out lunch specials in dialects I barely understood. We had trishaws instead of Ubers and neighbors instead of security gates. It was simple, messy, loud, and I loved it.

But the British left more than just their tea and traffic rules behind. They left us with a cultural blueprint for what it meant to be successful, educated, civilized, and female.

They taught us to sit up straight, speak the Queen's English, and never let our emotions get too loud. And my mother? She drank it all in. She made damn sure I did too.

When she could finally afford it, she signed me up for ballet lessons with Mrs. Eberwine, a porcelain-skinned expat who taught with the stern elegance of the Royal Academy. It wasn't about the love of dance. It was about posture. Presentation. Poise.

"Don't hunch," my mom would say.

"People don't like hunched-up girls. Sit straight. Look pretty."

Ballet, apparently, was for beauty. Piano was for class. And both were for one thing: marriageability.

I was being polished like a jewel for some future man I hadn't met yet.

I hated the piano. Played like a clown. Eight grueling years of barely passing my Royal Academy exams, but mom didn't care. I was her project. Her masterpiece. A girl who could dance, play music, walk into a room, and command admiration. Not for who I was, but for how well I could perform femininity.

Because to her, that meant I'd be safe. Secure. Married.

She wasn't trying to oppress me. She was trying to save me.

My mom grew up poor, the eldest daughter in a village in Kluang, Malaysia. One of nine kids. Her childhood was survival, not softness. Her father, a soldier, a drunk, a gambler, beat her mother bloody more times than anyone cared to count. She saw pain up close and clawed her way out of it the only way she knew how. She found a man who could take her far from it all.

And she did. My dad.

A Chinese man from Singapore. Business-minded. Ambitious. Stubborn as hell. And she, with her beauty and brains, was the perfect upgrade. She spoke English, cooked like a pro, cleaned like it was an Olympic sport, and looked stunning in photos. She gave him everything: her time, her energy, her skills, her body. In return, he gave her a secure life and a son.

That was the dream, right? A first-born son to carry on the Chinese name. Prestige. Worth. Purpose.

Then came the stillborn. A quiet devastation my mother never got to grieve. Back then, it was always the woman's fault. Like her body failed. Like she failed.

And then I arrived. Every step, every kick, every breath she took was wrapped in fear and quiet guilt.

And my dad? I was this little jewel that he didn't want to lose again. He was wrapped around my little finger from day one. I was his girl. His princess. His favorite. And my poor brother? He got the hard side. The pressure. The discipline. The distance. I got the softness. The smiles. The permission to be imperfect.

Of course, that lit the fuse of sibling rivalry early. But more than that, it laid the foundation for how I understood worth.

My mom was grooming me, not for independence, but for approval. And that approval would always come from men.

She taught me how to cater. How to serve. How to be desirable without ever needing to be heard.

She made breakfast every morning for my father. Ironed his shirts so crisp they could slice through arrogance. She pinched every penny. Cleaned every corner. Carried me in a sarong sling on her back while she worked like a ghost. Always there. Always invisible.

I was her mini-me. Her shadow. Watching. Learning. Understanding early that a woman's job was to disappear into the needs of her husband.

This isn't me shaming my mother. This is me understanding her.

She taught me what she knew. She was trying to give me a

better life than she had. That's the irony. She trained me to be a good wife, thinking it was a gift, but it was a cage.

Because no one told her the truth.

No one told her that being the good wife doesn't guarantee safety. Or power. Or even kindness. No one told her that even if you give a man everything, he will still betray you.

And my dad? He did. Over and over.

He cheated. He lied. He withheld. He treated her like a functional appliance. Something to admire, but not respect.

I don't know how I knew, but I knew. Kids always know.

I saw the loneliness in my mom's eyes. The way she stared out the window like she was somewhere else. The shouting. The silence. The sadness.

I also learned something else.

Being a good wife doesn't mean you'll be loved.

She couldn't leave. She had no money. No way to support herself. So she stayed. She endured. She yelled. She cried. Finally, she poured herself into me and said, not you too.

She made sure I had an education. Pushed me hard. Told me to reach farther than she ever could. Eventually, she changed. Her dream for me evolved from marrying well to stand on your own.

Unfortunately, the blueprint was already inside me. The muscle memory of obedience. The reflex to prioritize my partner's happiness over my own. The belief that unless there's physical abuse or an affair, you stay. Because that's what good wives do. That's what moms do. That's what love looks like. Right?

Except now I know. It's not love.

It's survival dressed up as duty.

And the worst part? I kept telling myself it was noble.

But now?

Now I'm starting to ask, what if I was never meant to be a good wife?

What if I was meant to be a whole woman?

3

THE ILLUSION OF PERFECT

"You can be the most beautiful woman in the room, and still be unseen."
—*Rupi Kaur*

When you're a teenage girl trying to earn love in a world that teaches you your worth is transactional, you don't question much. You just perform. And I performed beautifully.

In Singapore's glittering social landscape where status often spoke louder than character, it was an unspoken prize to land a wealthy boyfriend. A boy with a car, money, influence. That was the dream. That was security. That was a success. So when my first boyfriend, smart, sharp, and dripping in privilege, picked me, I thought I had won. My life would be smooth now. All I had to do was keep him happy. Easy, right?

He was everything I thought I wanted. Rich. Confident. Admired. The kind of boy other girls whispered about. I was the one on his arm. He made me feel seen, at first. It didn't take long before that feeling turned into something else. I began to vanish inside his shadow.

He controlled everything. What I wore. How I did my hair. Who I could be friends with. I let him. I confused his attention for love. When he said the sky was pink, I smiled and agreed. When he made fun of my thighs, I thanked him for being honest. When he said I was getting too fat, I worked harder at the gym. I was molding myself into someone he might find worthy enough to marry. That was the end goal, wasn't it? Marriage to a man like that would mean I'd made it.

But perfection has a cost. In my case, it cost me my voice.

The moment that cracked it all open came quietly, like most heartbreaks do. We had unprotected sex, and I got pregnant. I was terrified, and so was he. Not of what was happening to me, but of how it might ruin his life. He said he'd pay for the abortion, but he wanted nothing to do with it. No conversations. No hand-holding. Just get it done.

I never made it to that appointment. A few days beforehand, I miscarried.

It should have been a relief, but it wasn't. I was consumed by shame. I hated myself. Not just for getting pregnant, but for not wanting the baby. I didn't yet understand that I was a child myself, unequipped to carry another. I wasn't a murderer. I was a girl trying to survive. I carried that guilt for years. It etched itself deep into my bones. The Universe had intervened, but back then I didn't recognize its grace. All I felt was failure.

That miscarriage became my first moment of awakening. The rose-colored glasses fell off. I began to see him. Really see him for what he was. Cold. Conditional. Controlling. He didn't love me. He loved the idea of a girl who could fit his world. I was just playing the part.

The truth is, I had been emotionally abused. I didn't have the language for it back then. It didn't look like the dramatic stories I had heard. He never hit me. He never yelled. Emotional abuse doesn't always come with bruises. Sometimes it's subtle. Death by a thousand cuts. A backhanded compliment here. A withdrawn silence there. The look in someone's eyes when you realize they don't see you anymore, and maybe they never really did.

I stayed far too long. I thought I could fix it if I just tried harder. If I just looked better. Ate less. Spoke softer. Smiled more often. Eventually, the ache of being unseen, unloved, unwanted, wore me down. I was no longer a girl in love. I was a girl trying not to disappear.

He was already seeing someone else. That's what ended us, technically. But truthfully, we were over long before that. I just didn't want to admit it. The fantasy of our future kept me clinging. In the months that followed, I kept asking the same question. What did I do wrong? Why wasn't I enough? Was I not beautiful enough? Was I too loud? Too needy? Too much? It took me a long time to understand that it wasn't me. His inability to love me wasn't a reflection of my worth. My failure to meet impossible standards wasn't actually a failure at all. It was a rebellion waiting to happen.

He taught me something, unintentionally. He taught me that perfection is a myth sold to women to keep us small. I learned that if I kept striving to be good enough for someone else, I'd never be good enough for myself. When we contort ourselves to fit someone else's mold, we betray the truest parts of who we are. Since that heartbreak, I've spent years trying to unlearn what that boy taught me. Love should hurt. Beauty equals value. Silence equals peace. Pleasing someone else is more important than knowing yourself.

I was still learning.

But here's what I know now:

Love is not performance.

Worth is not earned by obedience.

And being perfect will never be enough for someone who doesn't know how to love.

So I let go of "perfect".

And I began the slow, painful journey of choosing myself instead.

4

THE GUY WHO CHEWED WITH HIS MOUTH OPEN

"I was looking for someone to dance with me in the chaos. Not someone who needed me to follow the choreography."
   —Atticus

I gave up dating "husband material."
   It wasn't working. I had tried the polished, respectable, highly educated boys that looked great on paper and passed every test set by my culture. But what looked right didn't feel right. What was supposed to guarantee love, security, and pride left me more hollow than whole.

After my last heartbreak, my parents started setting me up on blind dates. One in particular stood out. A smart, polished, Singaporean Chinese man who was a graduate from Stanford. The kind of man you could display like an award on a mantlepiece. We talked. I smiled. He nodded. I saw it all laid out: I'd have to shrink my voice, wear the right dresses, mind the right words, and surrender any dreams that didn't orbit around him.

No. No, thank you.

I ghosted him after one date. Maybe I should've felt guilty, but I didn't. For the first time, I was beginning to understand what I didn't want. That was a start.

Then, over gumbo and beer at a bar with some friends, I met Dean.

He was quiet at first, kind of shy. After a few drinks, his cracking jokes caught me off guard, and I laughed more in one night than I had in months. He introduced me to "Black and Tan," a horrid tasting mix of two beers, and he sat across from me, openly chewing his food, slurping down soup, completely unbothered by etiquette or appearances.

Not husband material. Definitely not.

And yet, he cleaned the bowl with a slice of bread like it was an art. I found that strangely attractive. Still do.

Dean was American, a white boy. I was Chinese. That alone meant everything and nothing, depending on whose eyes you looked through.

He wasn't the marrying kind, not for me anyway. Not for a girl raised in a family like mine. But he let me be. He didn't make me second-guess what I wore. He didn't care if I shaved my legs or folded the laundry on time. He didn't care about my thighs or my weight. He didn't expect a hot meal, a quiet mouth, or unquestioning obedience.

It was the most freeing relationship I had ever known.

He never told me what to do, and I never had to ask for permission to be myself. In a world where women were taught to shrink to make space for love, he made room for all of me. I didn't even know that was possible.

But to my family, Dean was the embodiment of everything I'd done wrong. Not because of how he treated me, but because he wasn't Chinese.

In my culture, marrying outside your race wasn't neutral, it was failure. It meant you were too flawed for one of your own. My mother worried for my future, my father grew silent, and my brother told me flat out he was ashamed of me. And Dean and I were just dating.

He was imperfect to them, but for the first time, I questioned what "imperfect" really meant.

I had tried "perfect." Perfect made me perform, starve, and shrink. Perfect nearly broke me. So maybe imperfect was the real prize.

Dean and I fell in love without trying. There was no performance, no agenda. Just late-night talks, accidental kisses, unfiltered laughter. I met him the night before my graduation from The Ohio State University, and two weeks later I left home for Singapore.

We tried to let go. We dated other people. We said we'd stay in touch. But I missed him. Missed him in a way that felt cellular. Every part of me remembered him: his laugh, his questions, his way of looking at me like I mattered.

After a year apart, I faced a choice: close the chapter and play it safe, or leap toward love with no guarantees.

Everyone advised the first option, but my best friend, bless her brave, sharp clarity, asked me one thing:

"If you married him, would it make you happy?"

Yes.

I didn't even hesitate.

"Yes."

"Then what are you doing here in Singapore?" She stared at me.

She said it so plainly. So powerfully. As though my happiness didn't have to be a complicated negotiation. As though I could actually choose it.

That question changed everything. Suddenly, I wasn't asking for permission. I was answering to myself.

Choosing Dean meant leaving my country, my family, my friends, and the only version of life I ever knew. It meant choosing the imperfect guy at the bar, the one who chewed with his mouth open and loved me without conditions. The one I wasn't supposed to marry.

But it also meant choosing someone who treated me as an equal. I realized this was the kind of imperfect I could live with forever. So I moved back to the US to be with him and attend grad school.

5

TWO WEDDINGS AND A WHOLE LOT OF WTF

" A *Chinese wedding teaches you two things: how much your elders love tradition, and how much jewelry you can carry before your neck gives out."*

—A modern bride's lament

Dean wasn't the type to drop on one knee, and I wasn't the type who needed him to. There was no grand proposal, no champagne-soaked engagement party, no viral-worthy moment. The word "viral" didn't even exist back then before social media. We simply decided we were it for each other. He called my father to ask for my hand because, well, I figured my Chinese heritage deserved some gesture, and that was as formal as it got.

At the time, I was knee-deep in grad school, finishing my master's degree. Dean was already working as a pharmacist. When I wasn't studying, we were roaming Kansas or the world, indulging our curiosity for the world and each other. Every day already felt like a celebration. So why throw another one just for show?

I was twenty-three. Headstrong. In love. And proud that I had found someone I wanted to marry on my terms. I didn't need a fancy diamond ring that cost him three months' salary. But I still got a small one, chosen by my dad, no less. It makes me laugh now, realizing how little thought I gave toward the marriage logistics. I didn't think those details mattered. To me, all that wedding fuss was just ego dressed in lace.

My focus was elsewhere. My thesis, my future, my independence.

"Why do you need a graduate degree? All you women are good for is getting barefoot and pregnant," my brother quipped.

It wasn't surprising. I was the first woman on either side of my family, maternal or paternal, to earn even a basic degree. In our culture, once a woman reached a certain age, she was married off. Education beyond that wasn't just unnecessary. In fact, it was threatening. A woman with a Master's, let alone a PhD, was either un-marriable or destined to die childless and alone. In traditional Southeast Asian Chinese circles, that's still seen as a kind of failure. It's heartbreaking, really, to be valued more for your womb than your mind.

But Dean? Dean saw me.

"If you want to do it, then do it," he said one night as I wavered over applying for a PhD. "You don't need my permission. Just be happy."

That sealed it. I knew I was going to marry this man. I knew it the way you know you've found your home. That's why I didn't need a big engagement. The partnership was already real.

Our official wedding? It happened quietly at the Riley County courthouse in Manhattan, Kansas. Just us, our two closest friends, and a small dinner at Harry's Uptown. Honestly, it's my favorite memory of our marriage. No stress. No spectacle. Just us, calm, happy, and totally present.

Then came the other wedding in Singapore.

"Red or pink cards? What colour flowers? What's on the menu?" My eight-month-pregnant BFF was trying her best to help me plan the Singaporean ceremony. I was exhausted just thinking about it. I didn't understand why dresses were so expensive or why weddings had to feel like a full-time job.

But my dad wanted it. The whole Chinese shebang. A Buddhist blessing, a traditional tea ceremony, and a 20-table, 10-course celebration. I'll admit, though, the economics of it were genius. In America, the bride's father foots the bill. In Singapore, it's the groom's. However, seeing that my dad wanted the celebration, Dean and my dad decided we would split the costs in the end. And thanks to the red envelopes stuffed with money from every guest, often with a 10 to 20 percent markup from the cost of a table, we made most of it back.

Then came the jewelry. So much gold.

I still have it all, and I have never worn it. I have no idea what to do with it. Couldn't they have just given me cash?

I'm not mocking the culture. Truly. I get it now. How jewelry signifies a woman's worth, and how it tells the world she belongs to a family of means. In the old Peranakan and Straits traditions, gold wasn't just bling. It was a status broadcast. So I honored that. I let my elders have their moment. Even if, inside, I didn't need it.

But nothing, absolutely nothing, prepared me for the pig.

"The pig's head is to be in your wedding suite tonight," my father told Dean, straight-faced.

In our tradition, a roasted suckling pig is a sign of status. My father literally pulled one off the wedding table and handed it to Dean, explaining that if the man is satisfied with his virgin bride, he keeps the pig's head. If not, he returns it the next day.

I turned to Dean and said, "I'm as virgin as a blank CD, so

that pig head stays the hell out of this honeymoon suite, or you're getting none of this."

We laughed so hard that night. It was fun, it was awkward, and it was us. The traditional "Yum Seng" at every table, all 20 times, made us drunk by the end of the night. Even amidst the absurdity, even while I complained about the money and the fuss, I knew one thing for sure. I had chosen the right man. Now, my family loves Dean and treats him as one of their own.

6

BREASTMILK, BOTTLES, AND A DISSERTATION

"Making the decision to have a child is... to decide forever to have your heart go walking around outside your body."
—*Elizabeth Stone*

Raised in the rhythms of Buddhist teachings, I learned about karma and reincarnation before I could even spell the words. My father, devout and wise in his way, passed down the Dharma like heirloom silk, precious and unquestioned. However, as I grew into my own questions, I began to sense there were deeper, messier layers to life that Buddhism didn't fully explain. I believed in purpose, in soul contracts, in something beyond the neat cycles of rebirth. I had always been spiritual. Curious. Hungry for answers to life's biggest questions. If money hadn't pulled at me so strongly, maybe I would have become a wandering mystic, the type who reads people more than books.

But education was my path, and I pursued it like it was oxygen. I didn't know how to get there. I only knew I had to. That desire took me halfway across the world to The Ohio State University, where I earned a degree in Food Science and

Nutrition. Later, I continued at Kansas State University, earning both a Master's and PhD in Grain Science, specializing in Baking. My dad paid for my undergrad, and the rest I hustled through assistantships. It was hard, but it was mine.

A PhD was never about prestige for me. I didn't want to be a professor nor a scholar. I didn't dream of white coats nor lecture halls. I simply needed to prove to myself that I could do it. I didn't have to explain why. It was a contract I came into this life to fulfill.

And somewhere along the way, I found Dean, my match, not because he accepted my education, but because he never made it a condition of love. He valued my intellect, my curiosity, and my warped sense of humor. He didn't care if I had degrees or not. He just liked me.

Right as I was preparing to defend my dissertation on a sensory apparatus for analyzing grain-based foods, our first son arrived. I was twenty-nine, finishing data collection, pregnant, and exhausted. The pregnancy had been strange: no morning sickness, but constant bleeding. I didn't know what was normal. I was just trying to stay focused and finish.

And then, everything shattered.

Our son was born with a congenital heart defect. Holes in his tiny heart. He couldn't breathe properly, and he couldn't suck from a bottle without gasping. He wasn't eating. He wasn't gaining weight. We spent the first three weeks of his life in the Neonatal Intensive Care Unit and Ronald McDonald House Charities in Kansas City.

Everything changed. My career ambitions fell away. My research, my carefully constructed career plan, none of it mattered. My son was alive. That was all I could see. Perhaps it was a divine intervention to veer me away from the research career in the private sector I was preparing for.

At six months old, our son had open-heart surgery. I cannot explain what it feels like to hand your fifteen-pound baby over to surgeons, to see stitches on that tiny chest, to watch tubes snake out of someone you grew inside yourself. I carried a guilt that never asked to be carried, the kind only mothers understand. This is why I am a supporter of March of Dimes and RMHC. They gave me hope and supported me. If you're reading this, and you're here in this space at this moment, I see you. You are not alone. It does pass.

And it did. Miraculously. Today, twenty-four years later, he is healthy and whole.

But back then, I was drowning. Postpartum depression. Sleepless nights. Constant feeding schedules. Fear. I remember bringing him home from the NICU, watching his chest rise and fall because I didn't trust life enough to do it on its own. I didn't know how to change a diaper. I didn't know when to feed him. He breastfed in short bursts, too tired to go longer than a couple of minutes. So we turned to the bottle. No guilt. Just survival. I could track his intake, and that gave me a sliver of control.

The anxiety didn't lift until he gained enough weight for surgery. It was a crash course in motherhood, taught by a fragile little professor with a broken heart. My children, as you'll see, tend to wake me up in brutal, but beautiful ways.

Looking back, if he had been born just a decade earlier, he might not have survived. We had no family history of congenital heart defects. We lived clean, healthy lives. I searched for reasons, then surrendered to the mystery. And in that space of searching, I found the start of my spiritual path.

I didn't abandon my PhD, but I did lose passion for it. With the help of my mother, who dropped everything to care for my son like she once cared for me, I defended my dissertation and walked across that stage. I am forever grateful to my mother and my professor, my mentor, who understood motherhood and gave me grace.

Defending my PhD remains my second greatest accomplishment. The first? Surviving that first year of motherhood.

My degree was a journey with clear steps and outcomes. Life is not. After that chapter, academia no longer called to me, because my son was alive, and that's all I cared for. While peers pursued research and academic careers, I pivoted toward something else, a life built around family.

That, too, was an achievement. Choosing presence over prestige. Choosing to live in alignment with what mattered and learning that control isn't found in doing everything, but in knowing what needs to be done and letting the rest go.

BURNED BREAD AND BROKEN DREAMS

"A fall from the third floor hurts as much as a fall from the hundredth.
If I have to fall, may it be from a high place."
　　—*Paulo Coelho*

This is what I call my Café Chapter, the one where I went all in. Where ambition and motherhood collided, and the dream of flexible entrepreneurship became the very thing that nearly undid me.

After deciding not to pursue academia, I longed for a path that would allow me to stay close to my family while still making something of my own. With the support of my parents' capital and a loan tied to our house, I opened a bakery-café in Cherry Creek, Denver, Colorado. I had always wanted one, and I imagined warm bread, community tables, and the kind of freedom that allowed me to pick up my kid from school in the afternoons.

I was in my early 30s, determined and bright-eyed, with a grand vision to invent a bake-on-demand system that could deliver hot, fresh bread in under ten minutes. And I did. I even patented it. My dream was to franchise it across the country.

What I didn't anticipate was how a retail business can consume you. My bakery didn't run me, it devoured me. I hired poorly in the beginning, making rookie mistakes as a first-time manager. Staff turnover drained my energy and my finances. I caught two employees stealing from the register, and I had to call the police on both of them. Others were honest, but food would go missing. Revenue stalled, and I found myself glued to the counter seven days a week because the moment I wasn't there, things fell apart.

At home, I was unraveling. I was pregnant again, working 60-hour weeks, emotionally depleted, and no longer able to show up as the mother or partner I wanted to be. I was always working on weekends, holidays, and birthdays. Eventually, shortly after my second son, Bear, was born, I had to make a decision. I shut the café down. I couldn't do it anymore.

It felt like failure. Now, looking back, I know it was a necessary fall.

Yet, amid the chaos, the café gave me something priceless. It gave me connection. Real, soul-deep connection. I met Sally there, who was my spiritual mother, my business coach, my white witch in lipstick, wrapped in sarcasm. She was an astrologer who believed in me more than I believed in myself. She predicted I'd succeed at whatever I touched, and she held me accountable for every decision I made. Sally died seven years after I closed the café. Her loss gutted me. But I still feel her. She became one of my fiercest guardian angels.

And then there was Gene X., a retired merchant captain, philosopher, friend. At the café's final dinner, Gene looked me in the eye and said, "You gave it your all, and I'm happy I saw it." I carry those words with me still. Gene, I miss you. May your spirit mingle eternally with Chiang Kai-Shek and sail freely through the tunnels of Guam, or wherever your soul found its port.

The café wasn't just a business. It was a crucible. It taught me how to really listen to people. It showed me that ideas mean nothing without grit, and that even if you walk away with nothing tangible, the wisdom stays. Ironically, years later, a large company bought the rights to my bake-on-demand patent. So, yes, in the end, someone did pay for it.

I didn't come out unscathed. Dean and I had tied our house to the business loan. When the money ran out and the bills piled up, we lost our house. We filed for bankruptcy. I was humiliated. I gambled and lost. Dean was mad at me, but he stood beside me through every crushing moment. The weight of that failure, as a business owner, wife, and mother, almost broke me.

It took time to rebuild. To forgive myself. To realize that entrepreneurship is not just about risk, but about resilience. This chapter taught me that dreams are worth chasing, but not at the cost of everything that keeps you whole. I fell hard. From a very high place.

And yes, it hurt like hell.

YOU CAN'T POUR FROM AN EMPTY CUP

"There is hope, even when your brain tells you otherwise."
—*John Green*

They say your firstborn is supposed to scare you out of having more kids. It took me three years to even consider pregnancy again after our time in the NICU, but then came Dr. Johnny Johnson. An angel disguised as a cautious, shoelace-tying, paranoia-soothing OB in Denver. He was the kind of doctor who picked up your call at any time, talked you off hormonal cliffs, and reminded you that your body wasn't broken just because your heart was tired. After Baby's traumatic arrival, I needed that kind of care.

Pregnancy with Bear wasn't easy, but it wasn't catastrophic. No morning sickness, a few scares of bleeding, and, like his brother, he had to be evicted. He was a healthy baby, no CHD. Just hearing that made me feel like I could exhale for the first time in years. Having a "normal" baby after trauma felt like being handed back a piece of the motherhood dream I thought I had lost.

Bear was a unicorn newborn. He ate, he slept, he cooed on

cue. But no matter how "easy" he was, postpartum depression didn't care. It came anyway. Creeping in during 3 a.m. feedings, whispering lies while I pumped milk in the back of the café. I was running a business, mothering two kids, and barely holding my own brain together. I cried while breastfeeding. I questioned if my milk was enough. I hated myself for not feeling more joy. I would think, "He's not gaining weight. It must be my fault. I'm failing. Maybe they'd all be better off without me." These thoughts were not logical, but they felt real. They felt like the truth.

I kept working. I ran a café while being crushed by depression. I snapped at customers. I lost connection with staff members. The business turned on me because I wasn't myself. I believe with all my heart that untreated postpartum depression helped bring down my business. You can't run a business if your soul is empty. When I finally told Dr. Johnson about my problems, he didn't hesitate. "Take the meds," he said. "They won't hurt the baby. And you need them. Also, sleep. Sleep is not a luxury. It's survival." He saved me. Not with prescriptions alone, but with compassion. He reminded me that it was okay to stop breastfeeding early, and that I wasn't less of a mother for needing help. I mattered too.

I had a dream: build a business that gave me freedom and let me stay close to my family. But I burned out. When the fog finally lifted, clarity came with it. I shut down the café. We packed up and moved to Zanesville, Ohio, to start over. Financially, emotionally, and as a family.

Let me be clear, burnout doesn't always come with sirens. Sometimes it sneaks in dressed as routine. You stop laughing as loudly. You stop dancing in the kitchen. You forget the sound of your own breath. That's how I knew I was empty.

In Zanesville, I learned how to be still again. I learned that motherhood isn't measured in ounces of milk or smiles per hour. It's in presence. In the ability to sit beside your child and whisper, "I see you," even when you're still trying to see yourself.

That year was the quietest chaos I've ever lived through. But I survived it. And I promise—if you're in it, you will too.

Just don't forget to pour back into you.

THE FIRST PIVOT

"The art of life is a constant readjustment to our surroundings."
— *Kakuzō Okakura*

The corporate life that my Food Science degrees prepared me for was meant to be stable, predictable, and structured. It came with a side of hairnets and safety goggles, and it promised two weeks of vacation a year if you were lucky. Most roles in food manufacturing were never designed with mothers in mind. They catered to men without caregiving responsibilities, or to women expected to pretend they didn't have any. But many of us didn't have that luxury—we had bills, babies, and no choice but to show up anyway. Still, after the café, after bankruptcy, and after my soul had been wrung out and hung to dry, I needed stability. So I stepped into the corporate manufacturing world.

Zanesville, Ohio, wasn't glamorous. It was a small town with quiet streets, working-class roots, and a job at a food manufacturing facility waiting for me. I thought maybe, just maybe, I could utilize my PhD in some meaningful way. I imagined clean spreadsheets, formulas, product launches, and adult conversations. I imagined a version of myself that could finally find balance.

I was wrong. It didn't take long to see that I didn't fit. Culturally, I was out of place. Too educated, too outspoken, too "other." My doctorate, instead of opening doors, seemed to make managers on the floor uncomfortable. When they found out I had children, the assumption wasn't admiration. It was judgment. The best thing I could do for my kids, they said, was to stay home. That message was delivered via sideways glances, awkward jokes, and the occasional unsolicited advice about my place.

But I stayed. I stayed because of my boss.

He was the VP of this manufacturing division, my manager, my mentor, and one of the rare humans who understood that leadership isn't about control. It's about vision. He made space for my motherhood. When I needed flexibility, he offered it. When I found out I was pregnant again, he didn't flinch. Under his leadership, I wasn't just tolerated. I was valued. He let me do what I did best. Innovate. He didn't ask me to shrink to fit. He gave me room to expand.

For many years, I worked under his guidance. We built sustainability initiatives, improved efficiencies, and found smarter and safer ways to produce food. It wasn't glamorous work, but it was impactful. In a small town where every job mattered, keeping the plant competitive meant keeping families fed. He knew that, and I got to help.

My time in Zanesville wasn't just about work. It was about rebuilding and learning how to be steady again after the chaos of entrepreneurship. It was about trusting myself in a new role. It was about healing.

During those years, Dean and I decided to try for a third child. I had just sold my patent, a tiny win after the crushing loss of the café. And what did I do with the money? I bought a Yamaha baby grand player piano that ran on floppy disks. It might sound ridiculous, but to me, it was a symbol of joy, beauty, and a little bit of magic. That piano sang life back into our home.

Not long after, Bee was conceived. From the start, the signs were familiar. No morning sickness. Strange meat aversions. And bleeding. Lots of bleeding. It was terrifying. I remember one episode so heavy, I thought I had miscarried. I called my boss in tears and went home to sleep. The next morning, the bleeding stopped. I realized I had slept on my left side all night, something I hadn't done consistently in my other pregnancies. From that night on, I committed to the left side. It worked. Bee stayed.

I share my story of pregnancy bleeding to let mothers know that it is okay to have occasional bleeding symptoms in pregnancy. It doesn't always indicate a negative outcome. However, do seek advice from your doctors. And yes, sleeping on your left side does help.

Following the footsteps of his brothers, Bee had to be forced out. He was born at nearly nine pounds. Healthy, beautiful, and perfectly content. He latched easily. Slept well. Rarely cried. He was our easiest baby by far. Breastfeeding was easy, and for a while, it felt like I was finally catching a break.

Unfortunately, postpartum depression doesn't care how easy your baby is.

This time, it hit harder than ever. Out of nowhere, I began having intrusive thoughts. Dark, unshakable, terrifying thoughts. I would be feeding Bee, watching his little fingers curl around mine, and suddenly wonder if the world would be better off without me. I would cry when Dean asked how my day had been. I felt hollow. Pointless. I couldn't feel joy. I couldn't feel anything.

Postpartum depression affects 85% of mothers to varying degrees. And yet, we barely talk about it. We praise the glowing mom with a latte, in Lululemons and a swaddled baby, but never ask how much she slept last night. Or whether she's eaten today. Or whether she's thought, even once, about driving away and never coming back.

Without support, postpartum depression can stretch out for months or even years. And yes, in the darkest corners of it, some mothers make unthinkable choices. Not because they're evil. But because they're empty. Alone. Desperate.

For moms out there: trust that this will pass. Your baby will grow. Sleep will return. Your hormones will settle. But please, when the baby sleeps, you sleep. Forget the dishes. Let the mountain of laundry become Everest. Sleep.

If you love a new mother, love her like you love the baby. Feed her. Let her sleep. Fold her laundry. Take her older kid out for pancakes. Depression doesn't always look like sadness. Sometimes it looks like silence. Irritability. A distant stare while bouncing the baby to sleep.

I had help. My mom was there. Dean was present. I had a job that wasn't crushing me. But none of that touched the storm within me. I didn't understand why I felt so broken, and that made me feel even worse. On the outside, I had everything. On the inside, I was drowning.

My doctor prescribed antidepressants. Within days, the fog lifted. It was as if someone had turned the lights back on. The suicidal thoughts vanished. My heart softened. I could finally love my baby the way he deserved to be loved. I could look in the mirror and not hate what I saw.

These experiences cemented something in me. Postpartum depression is real. It's hormonal. It's chemical. And it's treatable. There is no shame in taking medication. None. I have zero patience for those who shame new mothers into "toughing it out." If a mother is asking for help, give her the damn help.

We don't talk enough about what postpartum really feels like. We don't talk about the grief, the guilt, the disorientation. We glorify the glow, but we ignore the darkness. I had postpartum depression with all three of my children. It didn't matter how much I knew or how prepared I thought I was. It came anyway. I survived it every time with medication, support, and grace.

This is for the women out there who need to hear it. You are not broken. You are not failing. You are navigating one of the hardest things a human can do. If what you need is rest, medicine, help, or just someone to fold the damn laundry, ask for it. Demand it. You've earned it.

And this is for the men and partners. If your partner says she's not okay, believe her. Don't minimize. Don't fix. Just listen. Hold the baby. Make the meal. Give her a break. We gave life. The least you can do is help us hold onto ours.

My first pivot wasn't just professional. It was personal. It was learning how to show up for my family while still showing up for myself. It was learning how to be a mother to three boys, without losing my identity. It was learning that success isn't always about climbing. Sometimes, it's about staying. Grounding. Healing.

Zanesville gave me that. A steady job. A healthy baby. A chance to rest and rise again. It was then, for the first time in a long time, I started to believe that maybe I could do both. Be a mother and be something more.

Maybe, just maybe, I didn't have to choose.

10

MILK, CODE, AND A BABY GRAND

"Start where you are. Use what you have. Do what you can."
— *Arthur Ashe*

After the birth of Bee, I threw myself back into work with the kind of stubborn determination only a mother with three children and mounting bills could summon. I started back part time for six months, then returned full time. I was fortunate to have an understanding boss and coworkers who helped soften the jagged edges of juggling a newborn and a career.

Still, it wasn't easy. This was a time before nursing rooms and parental wellness policies were trending hashtags. I pumped breast milk in storage closets that smelled like damp cardboard, in bathrooms next to mop buckets, and once in a borrowed office where a well-meaning coworker barged in despite a very clear sign: "Pumping – Do Not Enter." My back was to the door, thank the gods of humility, but the damage to my dignity was done. I hollered, "Pumping! Be right with you in five minutes!" Just your typical Tuesday.

I nursed Bee for twelve months. The longest I had nursed

any of my boys. Baby got almost none. Bear made it six months. Bee got the marathon. What difference did it make? None. Absolutely none. They all got sick. They all got better. They all climbed trees, scraped knees, and survived my cooking. If I could go back in time, I would hand myself a hall pass to quit breastfeeding at three months and buy a year's worth of formula with zero guilt. So, to every corporate mom reading this: If you stop breastfeeding early, you're still amazing. Fed is fed. Sleep is life.

Despite the logistical circus and emotional wear, I stayed at that job longer than I expected. I wasn't working for the company. I was working for my boss. He saw me. He valued me. He showed me the numbers when our work improved efficiency. That kind of affirmation? Gold. But corporate politics started piling up like stale bread, and I had little patience for policy meetings and ego-driven roadblocks. Senior executives were wearing me out. I had three kids at home that were struggling for this time with me. I'd rather spend it with them, rather than trying to play the power game to climb the corporate ladder. I needed air.

So I quit.

I began writing a baking encyclopedia. Yes, you read that right.

At the New Bakery of Ohio, a high-output facility churning out baked goods by the millions, institutional knowledge was hoarded like it was currency. Veteran managers who had been there for 15 to 20 years didn't share anything. Not because they were malicious, but because they were scared. Their mindset was simple: If I keep the knowledge in my head, no one can replace me. No one can fire me.

That created a culture of gatekeeping. Only a few people were allowed to make decisions. No one dared alter a formula or touch a process. When I showed up, an Asian woman with a

PhD and zero tolerance for bullshit, the tension was immediate.

At first, I thought it was just due to unfamiliarity. Over time, it became clear that my presence threatened them. I represented change. Innovation. In their eyes, that meant obsolescence. What they didn't understand was that my manager, the visionary who hired me, brought me in not to replace them, but to elevate the entire operation. To innovate. To keep those manufacturing facilities competitive. To protect their jobs, not erase them.

I needed information. But no one was talking. So I turned to the next best thing: Google. However, in 2008, Google was basically a moody teenager. When I searched "ascorbic acid," I got tips for baking lemon cakes in your home oven. On page three. Business-to-business baking knowledge? Nearly nonexistent. Academic articles? Even worse. I realized then that the baking industry had a gaping hole in knowledge sharing.

So I dreamed up a solution.

I bought the domain. I wrote the first 100 pages of content myself. Everything from enzymes to dough conditioners. Just to show the concept. I pitched it to a trade organization. They passed. I pitched it to a trade publisher. They passed too. They were launching their own digital resource and saw me as competition. A one-woman threat with a domain name and a dream.

Their rejection lit a fire under me. I quit my job. I leaned fully into the vision, but I needed cash to make it real. This time, I didn't dare touch my house nor put our family into debt. I needed to do this myself.

So I sold my truck.

Then I sold my Yamaha baby grand player piano. My beloved, floppy disk-fed, self-playing beauty. Zanesville didn't exactly have a market for luxury musical instruments. So I called my friend in Cleveland: "Your kids will love this piano. And if they don't, it plays itself."

Boom.

Sold.

That money gave me my runway. My sacrifice.

I hired my first webmaster (yes, that was an actual job title back then, when websites were hand-coded and WordPress was still wearing diapers). I worked with my friend to create the first 300 pages. Another friend helped me navigate the alien world of digital publishing. Zanesville didn't have tech meetups or startup mentors. I had no idea what I was doing. I was terrified. But I kept going.

Google AdSense had launched in 2003, but it wasn't widely accessible nor effective for niche B2B sites like mine in 2012. Revenue wasn't flowing. Six months in, my bank account was a sad joke. I couldn't sell ads. I couldn't sell consulting. I was running out of money. Then the phone rang.

It was a recruiter.

A baking start-up on the West Coast needed a Director of R&D to scale their production. It was a lifeline. A shift. A nudge from the universe that said, "Nice work. Now get ready."

And just like that, we packed our dreams and prepared for another leap.

Because this wasn't the end of my digital resource.

It was just the rise before the real rise.

11

FROM KILLER BREAD TO CALLING

"Sometimes when you're in a dark place, you think you've been buried, but actually you've been planted."
— Christine Caine

"Is there really a Dave? Why did he name it Killer Bread? Do you know that 'killer' is not a good word to have on a brand? I've never heard of it. Oh… it's organic too."

That conversation, strange as it was, marked the start of a turning point I never saw coming. It was 2012, and organic bread was still a niche movement, a quiet hum in the background of the food world. Scaling organic baking into a high-speed operation seemed improbable. I was deep into my digital resource, not looking for distractions, but the recruiter on the other end of the phone was persistent. "Just go for an interview," she pleaded. They had been searching for someone technical.

Fine, I thought. What's one trip to Portland, Oregon?

I Googled Dave's Killer Bread before my flight and was impressed by the regional buzz. There were press articles and accolades, but no product on shelves in Ohio. I had never even tasted the bread. That alone made me hesitant. How do you interview with a company when you've never tried their product?

I walked into their bakery office, past a hallway lined with stories about Dave Dahl, his incarceration, his turnaround, his commitment to second chances. Then, a voice from behind me said: "So how did you hear about us?" It was Dave himself. Deep, raspy, real.

I panicked. I couldn't lie. I answered, "A recruiter told me you needed technical help."

I watched the disappointment flicker across his face.

Great start, Lady. Nice way to start a conversation with the King of Organic Bread!

I spent hours in interviews with the founders and their private equity partners. All amazing people, but I wasn't sold. Their operation was running slow with many changeovers, wildly inefficient by high-output baking standards. Why bring me in if they weren't even close to scaling?

Then Dave gave me the tour.

That's when everything changed.

We walked into the bakery, and it was buzzing with a maze of equipment, dough, and humans moving with purpose. The sheer variety of product SKUs (over 30!) was overwhelming. Still, I was unconvinced. But then Dave opened a walk-in cooler. He said, "We use refrigerated juice for our breads."

The scent hit me: fresh, tart, vibrant. Not from concentrate. Real.

"We get our freshly stone-ground organic wheat from Bob's Red Mill next door," he said, guiding me through rows of earthy, fragrant flour.

"And we sprout our own grains."

He opened a tank and let me inhale the scent of living wheat, sprouted and wet, brimming with energy.

Then he showed me how they ground the sprouts to make bread.

That was it.

I was sold.

Forget the numbers. I didn't care about their inefficiencies anymore. I was mesmerized by their innovation and commitment to ingredients, to process, to people. They were creating something authentic. Something worthy. I wanted in.

I was especially inspired by their second-chance mission. The idea of working with formerly incarcerated individuals didn't scare me. It excited me. I had never worked with the prison system before. I saw it as an opportunity to learn, grow, and contribute to something much bigger than myself.

"Do you need a rap sheet to work there?" a friend joked as we packed up our minivan for the move.

The job meant relocating the whole family from Zanesville, Ohio across the country to Portland, Oregon. Halfway through the cross-country trip, I had to fly ahead to start my new role, while Dean finished the drive alone with Baby, Bear, and Bee who were 12, 8, and 4 years old, respectively. Somewhere in the Midwest, a stranger paid for Dean's meal out of sympathy. Three kids, one stressed-out dad. A scene familiar to me but apparently more touching when the parent is male. I'd taken those same boys to countless restaurants solo, and no one ever picked up my tab. Double standards aside, it was a kindness we appreciated.

Part of my motivation for relocating was the school system. Lake Oswego, Oregon, was a major upgrade from what we had in Zanesville. But it came at a cost. We went from a $900 mortgage on a four-bedroom ranch on 12 acres, to a $3,100 rental for a three-bedroom townhouse far from the lake. We didn't want to buy at first, but two strong incomes allowed us to hire a nanny. We made it work.

At Dave's, I finally felt like I belonged to a company with

heart. I loved the team. The culture was inclusive. Ex-cons, single moms, career bakers. Everyone worked side by side. It felt like family. Scaling the business on the technical side became my responsibility, and I thrived in the chaos. It gave me purpose. Interestingly, while I was at Dave's, I developed an itchy red patch on my right shin. The doctor gave me a steroid cream. It came and went. I thought it was a gluten allergy from handling flour every day.

My digital resource took a back seat. We had run out of money in Zanesville, and it simply wasn't feasible. But I kept building it. At night. After work. Quietly creating pages, archiving knowledge, uploading what I could. I did it for the industry. I did it for my team at Dave's. I didn't know it then, but that act of dedication would become our lifeline.

Then a new CEO arrived. He was charismatic, brand-focused, and marketing-minded. I respected his strengths, but our values clashed. He prioritized image. I prioritized food safety, technical efficiencies, and operational truth. I wasn't flashy. I didn't play politics. I spoke my mind. My new boss liked things fluffy, polished, and wrapped in marketing gloss, but I preferred straight talk, clear facts, and getting to the point. We clashed.

In corporate America, that can be a death sentence. I was let go.

No drama. No theatrics. Just a clean exit.

It stung. Of course it did. But I understood. I didn't fit the new mold. I didn't play the team game. I had spent too much time trying to do what was right instead of what was popular.

Still, it broke my heart.

I loved that job. I loved my co-workers. I believed in that mission.

And yet, being let go turned out to be a gift.

With Dave's behind me, I had time again. I returned to building my digital resource. I poured everything I had into it.

The pain of being fired became fuel. The late-night content I had been creating? Now it had a home. Now it had my full attention.

Dave's Killer Bread was never just a job. It was a catalyst. It reignited my purpose. It reminded me that I'm not here to play it safe. I'm here to build. To speak the truth. To make the hard choices. To make something that matters.

Sometimes the door that closes is the one that frees you.

Sometimes the bread that breaks you becomes the bread that feeds you.

And sometimes, the killer part? That's just where the good story starts.

12

BOOTSTRAPS AND BREADCRUMBS

"Circumstances do not determine state of being. State of being determines circumstances. Circumstances don't matter. State of being does."
– *BASHAR*

I'd never been fired before.

When it happened, I didn't cry, scream, or spiral. I sat there and blinked. It felt surreal, like I had momentarily stepped out of my own movie. What was I supposed to learn from this?

Turns out, it was simple: Please your boss. Even if they're wrong, especially if they're wrong, make them look good. The secondary lesson? If you don't love your job, the Universe has a habit of dragging you out of it. Claw marks and all.

I came home and broke the news to the family. My son Bear clung to me, sobbing, "Mom, please, go and find a way for them to hire you again. I don't want you to leave Dave's. Please, Mom, please!". Apparently, he really loved them!

Honestly, I didn't even feel as bad as he did. He was more

heartbroken about the firing than I was. But the timing was a nightmare, just a week after we'd moved into our new house in Lake Oswego. If it weren't for my job, we wouldn't have qualified for the house in the first place. Now, I had some severance and a choice: panic or pivot.

I wasn't moving to get a new job in another city, which was required for someone with my specialty.

If you haven't lived in Lake Oswego, you might not understand the obsession. It's a postcard town. Safety, beauty, and serenity. A tight-knit, well-funded school system. Community events. Tryon State Park right in the backyard. Free access to the Willamette River. Parks and Rec is our second-highest city budget spend after police and fire. I know that because I once chaired the city budget committee. This place runs like a Swiss watch. We moved here for the schools, but we stayed because it felt like home.

Dean looked at me over coffee one morning, brows furrowed, "What's next?"

"Give me 90 days," I said. "I'm not going anywhere. This is our city. And I'm going to make it work."

We had a little in savings. Enough to carry us for a few months. We got rid of our nanny, as I took a machete to our budget. Dean leaned in harder at work, while I held down the home front. We knew how to live lean. We were raised that way. Rainy days come. This was a monsoon.

Here's the kicker. After I got fired, the rash disappeared. I didn't change my diet. I didn't change my detergent. I changed my life. Spiritually speaking, my body agreed with the change, and it stopped fighting with me anymore. In addition, we couldn't have gotten into this house if it weren't for my job!

In late 2014, I dusted off the digital resource I was working on. The domain had been quietly aging online for two years, which was a blessing in the eyes of Google's SEO gods. This time, I wasn't flying blind. This time, I was all in. I needed help. Real digital, tech-savvy help.

I marched into downtown Portland, knocking on every tech startup and incubator door I could find. PIE. TiE. Angel Networks. If they had a weird name and free coffee, I was there. I spoke the language of flour, not code, so I was completely out of my depth. Everyone wanted SaaS, Cloud, an app or some other acronym. No one cared about a B2B baking encyclopedia run by a forty-two-year-old mom of three. I pitched, and no one was interested in what I was starting up, because I wasn't going to give them their Unicorn exits. I wasn't even allowed in startup peer groups because I was self-funded, and I didn't speak their language of scaling, having traction, and the growth projections of hockey sticks. I joined start-up networking groups, and felt like the oldest person with the oldest technology in the room. Investors started talking to me, but stopped being interested when they found out I was married and had kids. I just didn't fit their mould of a young, vibrant, single founder without kids that would pour hundreds of hours per week into their investment. But then I caught a break. I joined a startup accelerator called TenX. It was costly, but it also changed everything for me, including my cash flow in 90 days.

Through TenX, I met Mark Grimes, the unofficial godfather of Portland startups. Mark ran a co-working space called NedSpace and had this uncanny ability to sniff out fluff in five seconds flat. He wasn't impressed by flashy decks or inflated valuations. He wanted grit, clarity, and vision. And he saw just enough in me to give a damn.

He didn't write me a check. What he gave me was better: time, mentorship, and a reality check. I asked for a free hot-desk at NedSpace. He looked at my logo for two seconds and chuckled.

He said, "If you're serious about raising a seed round, start by fixing your brand."

It felt like being slapped with a baguette, but he was right. I took his words seriously. I turned to my branding genius friend and I said, "I need this done. I can't pay you. Will you take ghost equity?"

To my astonishment, she agreed.

That's the thing about startups. They're built not just with capital, but with belief. She poured her talent into it, shaping our visual identity and brand voice. She made us the successful brand that we are. Meanwhile, I was wearing every hat imaginable, which was the writer, editor, salesperson, project manager, and administrator. During the day, I worked while the kids were at school. At night, I picked it up again when they were asleep. I had no formal training in digital publishing. I learned it all by doing it wrong first.

Blogs, newsletters, whitepapers, email funnels, social posts. It was content chaos. But it was also perfect timing. Content marketing was peaking. People were hungry for free, reliable, industry-specific knowledge, and I had it.

Six weeks into the TenX program, I landed my first sponsor.

One company believed in our mission. It wasn't a huge check, but it was enough to keep the lights on. I came home and waved the check in Dean's face like a lottery ticket. "I did it! And under 90 days!"

Momentum built. Within three months, I secured $50,000 in sponsorships for the coming year. Just me, a scrappy founder with an old laptop and no outside funding.

Every dollar went back into the company. I wasn't going to repeat the café mistakes. No bloated overhead. No expensive leases. Just lean growth and thoughtful reinvestment.

We grew from one person to three within two years. Then five.

I built slowly. I avoided debt. Every stumble became a story. Every mistake became a blog post. I ate 90 loaves of bread for 90 days just to show that you can't get fat from eating bread. It was a marketing ploy to get on stage, and it was successful, launching content in both audio and video formats. It launched my podcasting and influencer career. We were building something real.

Mark helped me connect with the right people. He helped me build a community of startup women. We organized pitch competitions and peer-support roundtables. We lifted each other up.

I had gone from being fired and flailing to building the largest digital baking platform in the world.

I was on my path.

I wasn't anyone's employee anymore.

I was the boss.

I was exactly where I was meant to be.

13

BETWEEN BEDTIMES AND DEADLINES

"The art of mothering is to teach the art of living to children."
– Elaine Heffner

At home, I made sure the kids got on the bus, then it was off to NedSpace for me. I could have worked from home, but being around like-minded individuals in that Portland coworking space energized me. Plus, I desperately needed the digital and marketing help that only such an environment could provide. I've always wrapped up work in time to meet the kids after school, then transitioned straight into sports, errands, cooking, showers, and bedtime routines. Dean sometimes worked weekends, so he'd take the weekdays to cover when I couldn't. We were stretched to our limits as a family. I hardly saw him.

Honestly, just writing about it makes me tired. The first four years of building this digital publishing company were a blur. While I originally built this company around my family, ironically, the more it grew, the more I was pulled away from them. Dean picked up the slack at home, often taking on the heavier load with the kids when

I couldn't be there. He stood on his feet for eight to ten hours a day at the pharmacy, only to come home to bedtime chaos and homework negotiations. We had to rework our schedules. Dean started going in later so he could handle mornings, and I picked up in the afternoons. We made it work.

Until Baby turned into a teenager.

His rebellion came out of nowhere and completely blindsided me. The yelling started. Homework wasn't done. Grades dropped. Curfews were ignored. And because most of it happened in the evenings while Dean was at work, I ended up blaming him for being absent. Our marriage, already strained by stress and exhaustion, took a hard hit.

Those were the years I thought about quitting everything.

But quitting wouldn't have magically made things better. Even if I had stayed home full time, we still wouldn't have had a two-parent household every night, the support that I needed, unless Dean gave up his job too, and that wasn't something we could afford. The pressure mounted until it finally took its toll: Dean lost a kidney to cancer.

That was a wake-up call I didn't want but clearly needed. It was a moment in my life that I was afraid for my children living without a father. Thankfully, the tumor was removed, and the cancer didn't spread. His cancer gave me a fright, however, it didn't affect or stop Baby's rebellion.

Spiritually, I believe I had been neglecting Baby. Not intentionally. I was afraid for him, and instead of leaning in with love, I leaned in with fear and control. He was trying to spread his wings, and I clipped them. I didn't trust his process because I was too distracted by everyone else who needed me. A partner recovering from cancer. Two younger siblings with their own needs. A company that required constant nurturing. There wasn't enough of me to go around.

But here's what I learned: Our kids are our greatest teachers. They hand-deliver us the lessons we didn't even know we needed.

I began to visualize everyone in my life as having a spiritual basket. Bee, Bear, Baby, Dean, and even my business. Each day, I had to top off these baskets with love, time, and attention. Each day, they would dip into those baskets, needing something. Dean and the business were easy. They were predictable. Bear and Bee were still small and manageable. But Baby's basket? That thing had holes! Every argument, every disappointment emptied the spiritual basket faster than I could refill it. When it ran out, he ran away. More than once.

In hindsight, I see that I tried to discipline instead of understand. I added more rules instead of more hugs. I set expectations when what he really needed was space to be who he was becoming. I was so focused on who I thought he should be that I forgot to celebrate who he already was.

To all the parents of teenagers reading this: Breathe. Trust yourself. Trust your child. Whatever you poured into them before they turned sixteen is already part of their foundation. They will draw from it when they need to. Let them launch. Don't clip their wings. Let them crash if they must, just be there to help them up. Don't try to steer their launch path. Let them choose their classes, their friends, and their path. Let them feel the triumph of navigating their own way.

And, no, it won't be perfect. It'll be messy and terrifying. But it's theirs. And it's necessary.

There were moments I wished I could have topped Baby's basket faster, fuller. But the truth is, I had nothing left to give at the end of those days. I gave everything I had, and I did my best. I carry no guilt for how he left because look at him now. Seven years of independent living, walking his own financial path, building his life. He found his way.

Baby and I look back now, sometimes together, and shake our heads. Why did we say those things? Why did we fight so hard? Today, our relationship is mending, slowly and steadily. He knows now that I love him deeply, not for what he could be, but for who he already is.

I believe we write our contracts before we are born. That we choose our parents, our families, our lessons. My soul tells me Baby chose us, me specifically, because he wanted to learn about fearless living, risk taking, and boundless love. I recognize myself in him, and that might be why we clashed so hard. It was like arguing with my younger, wilder self. I also believe he was the soul I miscarried long ago, the one who peeked into the future and decided to wait for technology to advance, and until Dean and I were ready.

And now, here he is. Living, thriving, and still teaching me.

That's what families do. We grow each other.

14

DIGGING FOR LIGHT

"In the midst of winter, I found there was, within me, an invincible summer."
— *Albert Camus*

After Baby left home, the silence was deafening. But not in a bad way. It was a return to stillness, a long exhale after years of walking on emotional eggshells. I didn't dread coming home anymore. I didn't brace myself at the door, wondering what mood would greet me. There was peace. An absence of shouting, tension, and sharp teenage energy. Dean must have felt it, too. No one barked at him, demanding justice from a sibling squabble, the moment he stepped through the door. We could sit down to dinner without one of us storming away mid-meal. For the first time in years, our home didn't feel like a minefield.

In Singapore, where I grew up, kids don't leave home until they're married. Housing is prohibitively expensive, and it makes practical sense for young adults to live with their parents until a couple's incomes can support a mortgage. Multigenerational households are the norm. You stay. You don't just take off after graduation. The idea that eighteen is the age of adulthood still sits awkwardly in my bones. But I was raising American kids, not Singaporean ones. I had to let that go too.

The feeling of Baby leaving was strange, a cocktail of relief and loss. I was relieved to no longer argue daily with a teenage boy in emotional chaos, but I was also lost. My identity as a mother had been wrapped tightly around him, his needs, his moods, and his future. Letting go felt like unraveling. There should be a post-baby book for this moment: "What to Expect When They Finally Leave." But there isn't. Just the ache, the questions, and a whole lot of soul searching.

You know that contract before birth I talked about? The one you supposedly sign with the universe, mapping out who you'll meet and what you'll experience in this life? Yeah, I wanted to rip that up. Who signs up for this much mess and complexity? Raising kids should come with a map. Being a wife should be easier. Running a business shouldn't feel like paddling upstream every single day.

Then COVID hit.

The shutdown didn't just change the world. It rerouted our family, our finances, and our mental health. My digital resource, went from in-person seminars and trade shows to digital everything. It was like flipping a switch, except that switch short-circuited half of our revenue streams. Employees got sick. Clients vanished. Sponsors paused contracts. Thank God for the Paycheck Protection Program, or we wouldn't have survived.

Working remotely became the new norm, but that also meant Bear and Bee were at home for school. I joined millions of other mothers trying to juggle work, tech support, teacher duties, and basic parenting, all under one roof. Dean, being a pharmacist, was a frontline worker. He had no options to stay home. Every shift was a risk, and every homecoming came with fear. We masked, sanitized, and vaccinated. I am still deeply grateful for the science that kept us safe. None of us caught COVID. That is a miracle I don't take lightly.

Emotionally, we didn't come out unscathed. Bear, who already struggled with anxiety before the pandemic, took a sharp downturn. Isolated from his friends, cut off from sports, and stuck behind screens, his mental health plummeted. Bee, too young to fully understand the chaos, also began showing signs of stress. There were tantrums, tears, and quiet sadness that hung in the air.

We needed a lifeline. That lifeline came in the form of a pop-up camper.

Camping saved us. That's not hyperbole. It gave us space to breathe, room to move, and the healing balm of the outdoors. Oregon and Washington became our playground. With our tiny trailer in tow, we discovered state parks, hidden forests, and BLM (Bureau of Land Management) lands that stretched into infinity. It was my first time camping with a hot shower every day, something that is required by a Singaporean woman used to city life.

That's also when I discovered rockhounding.

Rockhounds, by definition, are people who cannot walk by a pile of rocks without inspecting them for gems. That's it. That's the magic. One day it was, "Let's go to Richardson Ranch for thundereggs." Next, I was researching BLM maps, looking for mines, collecting guidebooks, and memorizing mineral compositions. What started as a fun hobby for the kids quickly became a full-blown obsession for me.

We visited Lucky Strike and Polka Dot mines for more thundereggs. Leslie Gulch for picture jaspers. Little Glass Butte for mahogany obsidian. Sunstones in Plush, opals near Burns, garnets in Idaho. BLM land became our treasure map, and the best part? It was free. No resort fees. No plane tickets. Just our trailer, our tools, and the wild terrain of the Pacific Northwest.

There's something sacred about being out there. No cell signal. No WiFi. Just the rhythmic scrape of your shovel, the gleam of a gemstone in your hand, the smell of sagebrush and dirt. These were vacations we could afford, emotionally and financially. State parks were cheap. BLM land was free. The memories were priceless and abundant.

In these wide-open spaces, we also discovered hot springs. The kind not found in guidebooks. The kind whispered to us by locals when we asked the right questions. After a long day of mining, we'd soak in thermal pools under the stars, surrounded by nothing but silence and sky. I wanted to show my kids how to forage and rockhound, and I hope they remember all our adventures in the wild.

Over time, the kids moved on. They grew older. Their interests shifted. But I didn't let go of rockhounding. It became my personal meditation. I started cutting stones, polishing them, wrapping them in wire to make jewelry. What had begun as a pandemic distraction turned into something much deeper —a creative outlet, a spiritual practice, a reminder that the Earth still gives.

Even now, years later, I still go rockhounding on solo trips. I bring my RV, some snacks, and my tools. I camp out on BLM land and lose myself in the rhythm of discovery. There's no reception out there, but somehow, I always find myself.

If you're a parent reading this, know this: You don't need Disneyland to make memories. You don't need an expensive cruise or a five-star resort. All you need is time, curiosity, and a willingness to get your hands dirty. The Earth will take care of the rest.

Rockhounding gave me something I didn't know I needed, which was a way to reconnect with my kids, a way to heal from burnout, a way to feel wonder again. It reminded me that even when the world feels like it's crumbling, there are still treasures beneath the surface, waiting to be unearthed.

Maybe, just maybe, we're all rockhounds. We're all just searching, digging, and scraping away at the layers of life, hoping to find something rare and beautiful to hold on to.

So go find your thunderegg.

Go find your spark.

15

BEAR'S AWAKENING, MY RECKONING

"It's okay not to be okay. It's okay to ask for help. It's okay to speak up for yourself."
  – Lady Gaga

W hen Bear turned seventeen, he changed. At one time, he would not like me to talk about this, but he has since grown out of this. I feel the need to share this because it turned my life upside down, and I want to help provide a roadmap for other mothers on how to deal with this pain. Mental illness affects all members of the family, not just the individual, and the best you can do without knowing much, is to stick together. Do not get into the details of who is to blame, because blaming has never solved any problems. Unify to support mental health care.

It was after a long camping trip in Eastern Oregon that we went back home to Lake Oswego to refuel and get back on the road. Bear didn't want to come with us because it was "too much family time" for him already. It was my mistake in leaving him alone for the next few days while we camped in Washington, because I thought he was a good teenager with good friends. Raising Bear so far had been relatively easy. Other than the common rebellious outbursts, he did well as a student, and he was outgrowing his anxiety. When we returned from the final camping trip, I noticed a slight change in him. Dean didn't detect anything, but I said there was something different. He was more agitated, his speech was faster, his eyes were all over the place. The next few nights, I noticed he turned off his lights later and later into the morning. He would be up later than me at night and earlier than me in the morning.

Back then, I was sleeping four to five hours per night. We were having issues with our marriage, mainly because I needed Dean at home at night with the kids, and he could only make that happen two or three times a week. I needed more help at home with a teenager, but asking Dean to quit his job to help me with this was too much to ask for. I also thought of closing my business to be at home, but that was difficult to do since that business engine was going, and it was going at a loss coming out of Covid. My frustrations and lack of sleep exacerbated my mental health and led me into a slight depression. All of a sudden, nothing was good anymore. I had the worst husband, I had the worst teenager, and I had the worst employees.

Little did I know, I had an underlying condition. On a regular health check, I complained to my doctor about a pain in my abdomen. He sent me for an ultrasound to see if that could pick up the issue. The abdomen was fine, and we couldn't see any physical issue. Then my doctor said, "You have a fatty liver, and your GGT is over the limit." My BMI was on the high side, and I don't drink alcohol. So what was causing this fatty liver? It was in my genes. My skinniest mom had non-alcoholic fatty liver disease (NAFLD), and so did

members of her family. With this knowledge, my doctor told
me to manage it by cutting deep-fried food and carbs, and to
exercise more. I was already doing my triathlons. I trained five
times a week, either on the bike, in the pool, or on the trails. I
did feel exhausted after each training, and now I know it was
the fatty liver that caused that.

That was the first time I joined a Facebook group for a
medical issue. The NAFLD Facebook support group (since
then, the disease has been relabeled to metabolic dysfunction-
associated steatotic liver disease, or MASLD) was supportive
and helpful in understanding this disease. It scared me to pieces
what some of these sufferers were experiencing, and I immediately planned to reverse it by changing my diet and fasting.
More on how I reversed this later, when I explain what
happened spiritually.

With my enlarged liver and not sleeping well, I noticed one
night that Bear hardly slept more than a couple of hours. This
seemed to go on for two weeks before he completely didn't
sleep at all. Looking back, I wish someone would have told me
to give him sleeping aids and work together with my husband
to get him to a therapist, to remove all media, and to get back
to normal sleeping patterns again. While it does sound simple,
I wasn't healthy, and I wasn't focused on meeting the demands
of this teenager whose hormones were what probably caused
the change in his behavior. My own spiritual basket was empty,
and Bear's wasn't filled, either.

The day his basket bottomed out, he got cited by the police
for riding his bike too fast and was saved by the police after
getting beat up at the park. Unusual behavior with police
touchpoints are indications of mental breakdowns. He was a
teenager who had never gotten into trouble at school, didn't
play truant, didn't do drugs or alcohol, and all of a sudden, a
change in behavior and the police with multiple touch points
within a day! I share this because I want parents to notice the

signs of mental breakdowns in teenagers and to take it seriously. I wish someone would have told me to focus on his sleep. It's where the answer is. We should have gotten the ring that kids can wear to sleep, to monitor his sleep before it all went downhill. Maybe he wouldn't have progressed to more serious episodes.

It was after the first episode in 2021 that our marriage went into the trenches. We didn't agree on medication. We didn't agree on therapy. I was struggling with my health, business, and family. It was like there was no end to my problems. Therefore, Bear's basket wasn't filled at all. We started fighting on medication, where Bear was insistent that he didn't need it because he wasn't sick. Then the second episode happened.

We were camping out of town, and when the breakdown started happening, he stopped sleeping, and that started his psychosis. All of a sudden, he was avoiding us and running away from us. His speech was fast, and his eyes were moving rapidly. However, this time he could control his words and convinced the police that we were bad helicopter parents controlling his every movement. During this time, I couldn't sleep because all I could think about was whether he would be alive the next day.

This is the side of mental illness that few talk about. The effect it has on family members is traumatic. We had very little to lean on. For family members who are new to this, please reach out to National Alliance on Mental Illness (NAMI) for support as soon as possible, get to know your local law enforcement, get enough sleep, unite, and be supportive of each other.

We really believed that if we were back home, the experience would have been different. We had mental health support systems in place, and our local law enforcement knew of us. However, having a breakdown on vacation in a foreign place meant we had none of that. There were no mental health specialists in the area we vacationed at, and because of that, I witnessed his painful breakdown over a span of many days.

It was like watching a stop-motion movie. You could predict every next moment, but you can't do anything about it. It broke every single part of my heart seeing Bear suffer like this. We couldn't get him into a car or on a plane to come back home because he was a flight risk.

Due to the lack of mental health support, we experienced so much blame from the police and health care workers as well. A few questioned if he was on drugs. One even said to me, "You really need to discipline your child. He shouldn't be talking to you like that." In addition, it's a California law that a child above fourteen years old has the right to refuse medication. Therefore, we couldn't force medication on him until he clearly showed signs of instability.

It took over 10 touchpoints with the police and four sleepless nights before they finally hospitalized him by force. That's when he totally broke down and experienced full psychosis. I was a mess at this point. Nothing could console me until he was confined within four walls and couldn't run out into traffic or get killed by law enforcement for running away. Not until I knew he was in the hospital, under care and medication, did I finally sleep.

When he was stabilized, after about five days in the hospital, he was released because there was a waiting list for incoming patients and not enough beds. I was mad at the world. Here is a really sick child that was being let go from the hospital without any support or follow-ups. If he had some other physical illness, they would have taken care of him and provided rehabilitation until he was well.

The health system in the US is so limited and ill-equipped in its ability to take care of kids with mental health issues. I cannot even imagine the lack of care for adults who suffer from mental health illness.

I've committed to sharing this story when I started writing this book so that others may learn from what I have experienced. I'm raising the red flag on teenage mental health. As parents, we need to allocate resources to this rising need.

The rate of increasing psychosis in children is alarming. According to a study published in the *Journal of the American Academy of Child and Adolescent Psychiatry (AACAP)*, approximately 12% of psychotic disorders and 8% of schizophrenia cases have onset prior to age eighteen.

This country has limited resources for navigating a teenage mental health crisis. The worst thing is that I see it and hear it more and more every day. Especially when a teenager is "acting out" on TV and social media. Now, when we see a teenager being documented as destructive, angry or violent for no reason, we understand that they could be going through the same illness as Bear.

Depression and suicide in teens are increasing at an alarming rate. The Centers for Disease Control and Prevention (CDC) reported that in 2021, suicide was the third leading cause of death among US high school youth aged 14–18 years, with 1,952 suicide-related deaths resulting in a rate of 9.0 per 100,000 youths.

Once this illness hits your family, your life will never be the same again.

Note: For those seeking support, the National Alliance on Mental Illness (NAMI) offers resources and assistance for families dealing with mental health challenges. Visit nami.org for more information.

16

THE CRACKS BENEATH THE CALM

"You never know how strong you are until being strong is your only choice."
— Bob Marley

Afterward, for the next few months, Bear struggled with school. His medication was too strong, and he had a hard time staying awake. He complained about not feeling like himself. We didn't know if he was going to graduate high school, or if there was another impending episode coming on. We had heated arguments about medication and therapy, and he was insistent that he was not sick. He was especially mad at me for talking about it, and for labeling him with mental illness. His graduation day was a deep sigh of relief for me. Not like how most mothers feel about their kid graduating and going off to college. I was relieved because he was alive to graduate from high school. I didn't care about college, I couldn't be happier.

During this time, Dean and I turned to NAMI and Life-works Northwest for resources. To this day, we are indebted to these two organizations for saving our son and giving us a somewhat normal life. A life-changing book that we read by Dr. Xavier Amador, *I Am Not Sick, I Don't Need Help!*, greatly changed our perspective on this illness. Thank you, Dr. Amador. Your book helped us navigate this challenging part of mental health and is a must-read for all families experiencing mental health issues.

When Bear turned eighteen during the summer after graduation, he stopped all medication. We didn't want him to leave the house, so we used all of the tactics in this book to continue establishing Bear's trust in us. To this day, we believe Dr. Amador's technique worked for us in keeping the channels of communication open with Bear. That was the calm before the storm in my marriage.

After the first episode, I didn't go back to being the same person again. My moods spiraled out of control as my marriage became a prison for me. Those were the times where every sight of my husband triggered a flight response. As mentioned in the beginning of this book, nothing he did was appealing to me. We tried marriage counseling. It was a very trying time for me as I cried, screamed, and yelled at him for the things he didn't know about. She was a good counselor in opening up the channels between Dean and myself.

The breakdown of our marriage started before Bear's episodes. I was overwhelmed with work, our house was getting old, and the large yard was overrun. Dean wasn't home enough with the boys, and when he had time off, his exercise on his bicycle took precedence over the kids, yard, and house work. When I tried to relieve him of the yard and house work, he would be mad at me. Once, I even paid a gardener to remove all our ivy that was overgrowing in our yard. He was furious with me for spending that money and didn't talk to me for days. He said we didn't have enough money to spend for this kind of work, but I begged to differ. I found the anger repulsive, then I found the house repulsive, but I understood that he was stressed about money.

Then Bear's first and second episodes happened, and I wasn't bringing in enough with my business to support the family. He felt it was his responsibility as a father to financially take care of everybody. Therefore, he had the upper hand with finances. It better go his way, or he would not be happy. I went through my life tiptoeing around the finance issues because I didn't want to make him mad.

You see, Dean was raised to save. His parents taught him not to get into debt and to be in control of every penny he spent. I was raised to honor and respect that the man of the house handles the finances, that's what good wives do. He was also frustrated that I didn't want to get a job that paid the same salary as his. Remember, when I mentioned that I loved Lake Oswego for our children and didn't want to move? That's the main reason why I didn't want to close my company to get a job. Getting a job also meant that I would have less time with my kids, and that wasn't my intention coming into this life.

So I thought, if we downsized, then Dean wouldn't be so stressed with our lifestyle and house payments. I wouldn't be so stressed with up-keeping a large house and yard, and I could just focus more on my business and children. Dean could even retire, cycle more, and have more time with Bear and Bee. That would be great for everyone, right?

Wrong.

The months leading up to his retirement, after retirement, and when we moved into our new smaller house, were the most excruciating months for me. If someone were to write a retirement guidebook for men, please include detailed chapters on how to find hobbies and friends before retirement. Also, adding a strong footnote on not moving houses would be helpful.

Dean didn't have good friends or drinking buddies because all he did was work, cycle, and spend time with his family.

That's very much a late Baby Boomer/Gen X trait. There was little socializing going on for him. What he had going for him was his cycling. It was what saved his health over the years, and it was now giving him purpose to get on the road to meet new friends. Remember, this is a guy who used to stand on his feet all day, working and interacting with people as a pharmacist. For him, this change was huge, and we weren't prepared for it.

"Why retire? He's so young," said many of my friends. Well, for one, I had been noticing Dean's health decline over the years. Being one of the frontline workers during COVID brought on the heartburn that never went away. Then, all of a sudden, more health care duties were placed unto pharmacists, and he's the kind of guy that would shoulder everything at work without complaining. This affected his sleep. The pharmacy scene was changing and evolved into something that he didn't sign up for 35+ years ago. Not forgetting that every day after work, he was but a shell for our family. He was there physically, but not emotionally on weeknights and weekends. So as you can see, retirement was going to be good for our family. However, he didn't see it that way. He immediately felt limitations in living the life that he wanted due to our cost-cutting lifestyle. He had to help plan meals, shop for groceries, drive to sporting events, help with household chores, and be a present spouse. He felt retirement should be like a cruise ship sailing into the sunset, but it wasn't. It felt like it was an upgrade for me and a downgrade for him. While he struggled daily to find his new rhythm, I could finally focus on getting myself healthier. It was during this time that I found the true solution to my metabolic dysfunction-associated steatotic liver disease (MASLD), and I will go into detail later when I talk about my body healing.

The arguments about duties and finances didn't stop. During one of the counseling sessions, I pointed out to him that this was how my dad controlled my mom. Financially and emotionally. I told him this was financial and emotional abuse, and I would not have it. He was disturbed that I said this, and he didn't know that his actions were perceived that way. No, I take that back. He didn't realize he was DOING it. This is what many of our mothers taught us: If there is no physical abuse, you should stay in the marriage because all marriages have some sort of control. My mom endured many years of it; her mom (my grandmother) did as well. It had to stop with me. I did not have to endure this.

When I told my parents that I was seeking a separation, they were shocked. They have never seen nor heard us argue. They asked, "Did he cheat on you?" No, neither of us were cheating on each other. Dean was a nice man, so I had to be the problem. They asked me to think deeply about it because it would affect Bee. I questioned marriage, the purpose of marriage, to its core. Was our marriage supposed to be for our kids? Are we staying together to make them feel happy and loved? That's not right. Why are two angry and miserable people staying together for children that we cannot ultimately control?

I did not believe in giving the control of my happiness to anyone else but myself. I control my own happiness, and it's not dependent on my children nor my husband. I believe it's the same way with them as well. They are going to be fine.

So why stay married? Is it for legal purposes? Now, this excuse was what kept my parents miserably married for decades. I did not intend to stay in my marriage because it was too legally expensive and monetarily difficult to separate. I would have done it in a heartbeat if it meant slicing our net worths into two halves. I didn't feel money should control me. I still don't. I can make it on my own.

So I asked myself again, why stay in a marriage that makes you miserable? Ego? Nope, I don't care about what people think of a divorcee. Convenience? Yeah, it's more convenient to stay married, but that's not a good reason either. Hope? To just pretend hard and long enough that it would all go away? Yeah, hope and I aren't best friends. Love? I think we had crossed that bridge, and it had since broken. I didn't love the man anymore but...

Friendship? That. It stopped me in my tracks. I had to think about that for a long while. He is a good person. A good friend. But you know what? Good friends can survive a divorce. I tore down my marriage into building blocks and found nothing that held it together. There was no logic for me to stay in this relationship anymore. Our marriage was so ruined that on our 25th wedding anniversary he didn't even plan anything special for us. I was upset. His reason was that we didn't have the money to do anything out of the ordinary. I felt that you don't need to spend much money to pull the trailer out to a nice park and have a candlelight dinner. That's how far apart we were in our feelings and emotions.

A few months after Bear's second episode, we couldn't agree on medication and therapies because we were so miserable with each other. I found a day where we were both calm and non-confrontational. The sun was out, and I brought him onto our patio because I wanted to have a relaxed conversation under our trees where the birds were chirping.

17

THE CONVERSATION THAT CHANGED EVERYTHING

"And the day came when the risk to remain tight in a bud was more painful than the risk it took to blossom."
— Anaïs Nin

"I want a divorce," I said to him.

He stared at me blankly, his eyes wide and unblinking, as the words slowly processed. For what felt like an entire hour, he didn't say anything. Silence stretched out between us, a dense, unmoving thing. I could see the calculations racing through his mind, not just the logistics of a divorce, but the emotional implications, the unraveling of a life we had stitched together over decades.

He finally let out a breath, slow and ragged. "Okay," he said softly. And just like that, something inside both of us shifted.

There were no screaming matches, no doors slammed, no storming out. Instead, we sat together, like business partners preparing to close a company. For the next few hours, we talked. Really talked. About who would keep the house, what would happen to the kids, how the holidays would look, and what it might feel like to date other people again. The absurdity of that part made us laugh through our tears, imagining ourselves swiping through dating apps or meeting someone new after all these years. It was surreal.

Then I told him something I had never admitted out loud: "We still have time. We're young enough to love someone else for the next 20 to 30 years. So if we need to go, we should go now, while we can still do it with grace, while we can still wish each other well."

It was a sobering truth. It changed the course of everything that followed.

Something clicked in that moment for the both of us. If we were willing to go through all the trouble of presenting our best selves to new people, then why weren't we willing to do that for each other? Why would we give our best to strangers but give crumbs to the person we built a life with?

That question hung in the air like a mirror, reflecting everything we had lost, but also everything we still had.

So we made a list. Not a list of grievances or unmet needs, but a list of things we could do to show up for each other again. What would it look like if we dated each other? If we tried to impress each other again?

For him, it meant more than just cycling less. It meant showing up emotionally, physically, and with presence. For me, it meant softening, listening, and letting go of resentment that had calcified in my bones. It meant being honest and brave in love again.

That night, after hours of talking, we embraced each other like we hadn't in years. Not the obligatory peck on the cheek or the distracted side hug in the hallway. We held each other like people who remembered what it felt like to be chosen.

And we cried.

Tears for the years lost to parenting struggles, financial anxiety, unresolved trauma, and unspoken needs. Tears for the hurtful things we had said, and for the quiet things we never said that hurt just as much. But we also cried for the possibility of a future that still included each other.

In many ways, that conversation was the real beginning of our marriage.

For years, we had been playing roles: husband, wife, parent, and provider. We followed the script. We performed for society, our families, and our friends. But we weren't showing up for each other, and we certainly weren't showing up for ourselves.

That night, on that patio with the birds chirping and the sunlight streaming through the trees, we tore up the script. We decided to write a new one, together.

This wasn't about pretending everything was fine. It wasn't about sweeping issues under the rug or settling for less than we deserved. It was about seeing each other clearly and choosing each other, flaws and all.

We set ground rules. No weaponizing past mistakes. No scorekeeping. Daily hugs and kisses. Real date nights—not the kind where we go to the grocery store without the kids, but actual moments of connection.

Something remarkable happened.

We began to heal.

It wasn't linear. There were setbacks. Disagreements. Moments when I still wanted to walk away. But I saw progress. There were long walks, honest talks, belly laughs, and quiet mornings drinking coffee together without tension.

I started to fall in love again.

Not with the fantasy of who I thought Dean should be, but with the actual man and life in front of me. The man who listened when I spoke, who tried even when it was hard, who admitted when he was wrong, and who held me when I needed holding. Although he didn't change much, he tweaked his responses, and so did I. We both started to treat each other differently.

And Dean? He began to see me again—not just as the mother of his children or the woman managing the house, but as a partner, a person, a woman worthy of tenderness. He saw the good wife exit, and someone who is stronger and more honest replacing her.

We weren't perfect. We still aren't. But we are present. We are trying.

That conversation saved us. Or maybe it resurrected us.

I believe every marriage or long-term relationship hits a point where it needs to either dissolve or evolve. Ours evolved.

It took raw truth, deep respect, and the willingness to burn down what wasn't working in order to rebuild something better. We had to look at each other, not with resentment, but with curiosity. Who are you now? Who am I with you?

That day on the patio was the moment everything changed. It was the point where the story of us could have ended, but instead, it began a new chapter. One with less pretending and more presence. Less duty, more desire. Less fear, more faith.

So if you're reading this and you're on the brink of your marriage, know that the brink isn't the end. It's the beginning of the truth.

Sometimes speaking that truth out loud, even if it terrifies you, is the first step to everything you have been longing for.

That's what it was for us. That's what it can be for you.

The day I said "I want a divorce" was the day the good wife exited and I reclaimed my life. Paradoxically, it was the day our marriage came alive again.

That's what makes this chapter the turning point—not just in our marriage, but in my journey back to myself.

10 Tips for Starting a Transformative Conversation with Your Partner

1. Choose a warm, quiet room or a patio on a pleasant day. The setting should feel safe and open.

2. Pick a calm, neutral time to talk—about three to four uninterrupted hours. Avoid high-stress moments.

3. Say "I want a divorce." Speak from your heart, not your anger. Be honest, vulnerable, and use a welcoming tone, as if you're meeting someone new.

4. Start with what you want, not just what's wrong. Focus on dreams and needs, not just frustrations.

5. Listen to understand, not to reply. Be present and open, even when it's uncomfortable.

6. Avoid blaming language. Use "I feel" statements instead of "You always…" to reduce defensiveness.

7. Explore both possibilities: to dissolve or evolve. Lay them on the table with fairness and clarity. Talk through those two scenarios.

8. Allow silence. Let it stretch. Let the truth land. Let the heart catch up.

9. Reach a conclusion with 100% buy-in from both of you—not 80%, not 95%. All in or keep talking.

10. Hug. A full-body, no-ego bear hug. Then forgive with your whole heart.

18

WOUNDS THAT WON'T HEAL

"Trauma creates change you don't choose. Healing is about creating change you do choose."
    — Michelle Rosenthal

After Bear graduated from high school, he went to college for a semester. Living in the dormitory, adjusting to a roommate, and managing his academic workload quickly wore him down. He struggled to sleep, and the anxiety about performing in a college setting only worsened things. Going to college wasn't the path he wanted. I pressed on anyway, insisting he pursue continuous learning. I was holding tightly to the belief that education after high school would offer him stability, structure, and purpose. But all of it unraveled quickly. It wasn't what he wanted, and I had to face the guilt of pushing him in a direction he had never chosen for himself.

To show us that he could be fine on his own terms, he rented a small apartment in downtown Portland and got a job as a security guard. He wanted us to see that he could build a life with structure and intention. For a few months, it looked like he was right. He showed up to work, paid his rent, and maintained a routine. Dean and I started to exhale. Maybe, just maybe, the worst was behind us.

But then things started to shift. Bear became impulsive. He suddenly bought a car, draining his savings in one swoop. He told us it was for a job he was going to get in the near future, a job that hadn't yet materialized. Within weeks, he quit his security job without much explanation. When we asked him to come home, he agreed without any resistance. That was when my alarm bells started ringing. It felt like a child coming to their mother when they're feverish, seeking comfort and safety. I had a lump in my throat for days. Deep down, I knew we were nearing another episode. I didn't know when, but I could feel the dam beginning to crack.

"Mom, I'm driving to Corvallis to see a friend," he said one afternoon.

Those were the last words I heard before Bear went missing.

I couldn't stop him. He was legally an adult. He owned his car. He had the right to go wherever he wanted. I couldn't take anything away from him. He had full autonomy, and I had to learn how to sit with that reality. It was my first real lesson in letting go. But I didn't understand that until later, when I met my hypnotist. More on that session to come.

In the past, Bear had always blamed us for intervening. For chasing him, for calling the cops, for landing him in hospitals. This time we made a painful choice. We didn't chase him. We waited. We let him hit bottom, hoping it would finally make him open to receiving help.

After twenty-four hours of no contact, we started calling police departments all over Oregon. Nothing. It wasn't until the third day that we received a call. A police officer told us Bear's car had broken down and they had put him in jail to "sober up." Not because he was intoxicated, but because they didn't know what else to do. That's when we knew. He was unraveling again. When Bear went into psychosis, he didn't need drugs or alcohol to act erratically. The symptoms alone were enough.

This is where the system fails so many people. Law enforcement officers, ER staff, even first responders are not properly trained to recognize psychosis in young adults, especially those without a prior history of substance abuse. A psychotic episode often mimics intoxication, but it requires completely different treatment. Instead of getting him the care he needed, they treated him like he was drunk. They let him go the next day because he didn't meet the criteria for a psychiatric hold. He wasn't deemed a threat to himself or others, so they had no legal grounds to keep him.

At least we knew where he was. He was alive. However, the waiting game resumed. Eight separate interactions with the police would occur before Bear was finally hospitalized. Eight. Each one draining, traumatic, and avoidable. If even one of those officers had been trained to recognize what was happening, Bear could have received care days earlier. I shudder to think about the wasted time, the wasted resources, the compounded trauma, for him and for us.

We drove down after the fourth incident, when he landed in the emergency room. Dean and I hoped that maybe, this time, he would be admitted. But Bear was still lucid enough to decline care. In Oregon, like in many states, adults must consent to treatment unless they meet strict criteria. So we left him there. We drove back home, completely helpless, praying for a miracle.

We knew bringing him home in our car was not an option. When he's in psychosis, he's a flight risk. We had experienced it before, the sudden bolt out of the car, the need to escape. I've often thought, if it were legal to sedate him just for the ride home, I might have done it. That's how desperate we were. But it isn't legal, and thank God for that. Because as painful as it was, Bear needed this journey. He needed to learn from it. Interfering might have interrupted a vital lesson.

Finally, nine days after he disappeared, Bear was admitted into a psychiatric ward. Nine days of uncertainty, nine days of not knowing if he would hurt himself or get hurt by someone else. It was a paper cut on top of a paper cut, invisible to the world, but a searing pain for me. It split open a wound in my heart that refused to close.

Perhaps that's the purpose of this journey, to feel this pain, to understand it intimately, and to use it to spread love and compassion for others going through it. When Bear came home two weeks later, he immediately stopped his medication again. But this time, we were ready.

We had learned about Anosognosia, the lack of insight commonly found in people with mental illness, from Dr. Amador's book. We started using the LEAP method: Listen, Empathize, Agree, and Partner. It worked. It didn't fix everything overnight, but it helped Bear trust us again, especially his father. For the first time in months, there was the faintest glimmer of hope.

Still, I needed more. I needed something deeper than medicine and method. I needed to find meaning in the suffering.

As a spiritual person, I believe there are lessons embedded in every hardship, opportunities folded into every pain. And I was desperate to understand what Bear's suffering was trying to teach me.

Around this time, I began reading Dolores Cannon's *The Convoluted Universe* series. It blew my mind wide open. Dolores's work, based in deep hypnosis and past-life regressions, told stories of people accessing their Higher Selves to answer their life's biggest questions. I devoured every page, hungry for spiritual truth and fascinated by the unknown.

One afternoon, I asked myself: What if hypnosis could help Bear? What if it could help us understand the root cause of his suffering? Unlike traditional therapy or medication, hypnosis is non-invasive. It doesn't require compliance. It doesn't require belief. It only requires openness.

So I started researching hypnosis. At first, I was overwhelmed. There were so many modalities, so many voices. I didn't know which path to follow. Then, while finishing *The Convoluted Universe: Book Three*, I learned that Dolores Cannon had created her own technique called Quantum Healing Hypnosis Technique (QHHT®). At the time of writing this book, it is currently being taught by her daughter, Julia Cannon.

My heart nearly exploded with excitement. This was it. This was the next step. But before I committed to taking the course, I needed to try it myself. I had never been hypnotized before. If I didn't like the experience, I knew it wouldn't be right for me.

I searched the QHHT® practitioner directory and found a Level 3 practitioner named Tracie Mahan near Portland. Level 3 meant she had undergone the highest level of certification, and that reassured me. If I was going to dive into this, I wanted to do it with someone deeply experienced. Selfishly, I was hoping I would get to meet my subconscious during the session and ask about Bear. I was desperate for answers.

When I booked the appointment with Tracie, I had no idea how transformational it would be. I only knew I was being pulled toward it, like a soul who had been waiting for this moment.

I remember telling myself, "Just go in with an open heart. Don't resist. Don't overthink. Let it unfold."

What happened next was nothing short of profound.

But that, dear reader, is a story you will read next.

PART 2

THE SOUL I CAME HERE TO BE

19

THE SCIENCE BEHIND THE MAGIC

"The day science begins to study non-physical phenomena, it will make more progress in one decade than in all the previous centuries of its existence."

-Nikola Tesla

Growing up in a Buddhist household, I was introduced early to the concepts of reincarnation, karma, and realms of existence beyond what we perceive with our five senses. These ideas were not fantasy nor metaphor; they were presented as truths that coexisted alongside the mundane world. I didn't grow up fearing death the way many others did. Instead, I saw it as a transition, a doorway. The belief that we have lived many lives, and will live many more, shaped my understanding of purpose and pain. So when I encountered the work of Dolores Cannon, it didn't seem far-fetched; it felt like a homecoming.

But despite my upbringing, I still became a scientist. I was trained in data, formulas, and evidence. I earned a PhD. I spent years solving industrial problems using logic and method. I believed in the power of proof. Which is why, when I started diving into QHHT®, I found myself at a strange crossroads between what I had been taught in school and what I had always felt in my bones.

At first, it felt like I had to choose. Either be the scientist or be the mystic. Either operate in the measurable world or the mysterious one. But the more I studied consciousness and quantum healing, the more I realized something profound: the line between science and spirit is thinner than we think.

Dolores Cannon (1931–2014), a pioneer in the field of past life regression and hypnosis, developed the Quantum Healing Hypnosis Technique® (QHHT®). Through her sessions and countless hours of transcription and research, she unearthed extraordinary accounts from clients under hypnosis. Stories of lives lived on other planets, encounters with higher beings, and soul contracts mapped out before birth. Dolores dared to go where few researchers ever tread. Her sessions pushed the boundaries of what we accept as real, and she did it all with curiosity, conviction, and a grounded sense of purpose. Her courage to share what others would label as "too out there" earned my respect, and my fascination.

As someone who is a scientist by nature, I don't follow things blindly. My approach to anything extraordinary begins with skepticism and a desire for measurable outcomes. What made Dolores' work stand out to me wasn't just the mysticism, it was her method. She documented her findings, looked for patterns, and approached her work as a researcher would. This resonated deeply with me. I found myself drawing parallels between her method and the principles of quantum mechanics, a field that also challenges our understanding of reality.

Quantum mechanics, at its core, is the study of particles at the smallest scale. It tells us that matter behaves both as particles and waves, that particles can exist in multiple states at once (superposition), and that merely observing a particle can change its behavior (the observer effect). None of this makes

sense in our classical, everyday understanding of the world, yet
it is demonstrably true. These principles are supported by
decades of rigorous experimentation and peer-reviewed
research. Yet, they sound more like science fiction than science
fact.

When I look at Dolores Cannon's work, particularly the
idea of accessing the subconscious through hypnosis to retrieve
information from past lives or higher dimensions, it feels
strangely familiar. In her program, people report experiences
that can't be explained by traditional psychology or medicine,
yet they often emerge from sessions healed, emotionally lighter,
or with new insight. From a scientific lens, it reminds me of the
uncertainty principle in quantum theory. Just because we can't
measure something directly doesn't mean it isn't real.

If quantum mechanics has taught us anything, it's that
reality is not as fixed nor logical as we once believed. There is
room, perhaps even necessity, for alternative ways of understanding. In this program, Dolores tapped into a hidden field
of consciousness, a layer of human experience that traditional
science hasn't yet caught up with. But just because science
hasn't defined it, doesn't mean it doesn't exist. As Arthur C.
Clarke famously said, "Any sufficiently advanced technology is
indistinguishable from magic."

In neuroscience, there are five primary brainwave frequen-
cies that represent different states of consciousness:

Frequency Band	Frequency Range	Associated Mental States and Functions
Gamma (γ)	30–100 Hz	High-level cognitive functioning, information processing, and consciousness.
Beta (β)	12–30 Hz	Active thinking, focus, problem solving, and alertness.
Alpha (α)	8–12 Hz	Relaxed meditative state, and a bridge between conscious and subconscious states.
Theta (θ)	4–8 Hz	Deep relaxation and access to the subconscious.
Delta (δ)	0.5–4 Hz	Deep sleep stages (NREM), unconsciousness, and restorative processes.

Theta is where the magic of hypnosis happens. It's a liminal state, one foot in the waking world, one foot in the subconscious. Dolores taught that, in this state, you could access the Subconscious Consciousness (SC), also known as the Higher Self. It's here that answers to your deepest questions reside. In the Theta realm, people uncover lifetimes they've forgotten, retrieve emotional memories buried under trauma, and even receive physical healing.

As a scientist, I relate to this as a consciousness-based quantum field. Our consciousness may very well function like quantum particles; it is non-local, nonlinear, and interconnected across time and space. The SC, then, could be a kind of observer, like a quantum-aware entity that collapses probability into reality. It sounds outlandish until you consider that quantum computers are built on similar ideas of superposition and entanglement. Why should our consciousness be any different?

If I had to describe Theta visually, I would compare it to walking through an interactive dreamscape like Meow Wolf. Strange, colorful, unpredictable, and undeniably real to the senses. Side note: One of my clients once told me, only half-jokingly, that she was irritated with me for pulling her out of the Theta state during our session. It was just so peaceful there. She didn't want to come back.

Getting into Theta is surprisingly easy. Our minds slip into it naturally every day as we drift to sleep and awaken. But staying there is the tricky part. That's what makes Dolores' method special. It's a structured, guided path that holds the door open to the subconscious long enough for insight, healing, and transformation to occur. That structure, the secret sauce, is what made me eager to try it for myself. I wasn't just intrigued. I was ready.

I share this story not to convince anyone of the technique's validity, but to offer a window into what can happen when you step beyond your conscious mind and into the realm of the subconscious. For those curious, skeptical, or afraid, I hope this glimpse encourages you to see it for what it is: a safe, expansive, and deeply personal journey inward.

The next chapter will take you through my wild ride with Tracie. Buckle up. It's going to be illuminating.

20

BETWEEN REALMS AND REASONS

"Science is not only compatible with spirituality; it is a profound source of spirituality."
—*Carl Sagan*

I really thought it was weird having a four- to five-hour session with a stranger. After all, what are we going to talk about? However, once Tracie got me talking, I realized there's so much of my life to unload. No one had ever asked me those questions before, and no one had ever taken the time to dig into my life. I felt seen, and I also felt very comfortable. When I started talking about Bear and how fearful I was for his life, tears flowed uncontrollably. It showed me that this wound was still open and it needed to be healed. I was able to prepare a list of questions, and I had to limit myself. Four areas of my life that I really wanted to explore were my children, my health, my marriage, and my business. The following is my journey from one session with her, and the hypnosis portion was recorded.

HYPNOSIS

After the interview, I got onto her bed, and no sooner, I felt like my body was floating in midair. It was such a wonderful feeling. To be without a body and just float with my arms hanging in mid air. This was my first experience with Theta realm, and it's just like what my clients always say, an-out-of body experience that makes you feel like you are floating with beautiful images all around you. How am I not making this up? Well, one thing is for sure, I have never floated. Not in my meditations, and definitely not in my sleep (I sleep like a log, and I mostly can't remember my dreams). Second, I can't make sh** up like that!

PAST LIFE REGRESSION

Tracie took me back to a past life as a child being abandoned in a mine. When I was exploring this as a little girl in bare feet, I needed guidance to describe the mine and the train shafts, as I have never seen these structures before. When Tracie asked where my parents were while I was playing in that mine, an immense pain went through my heart. It hurt and I cried, but Tracie relieved my pain through her magical words. My SC was protecting me from the visuals and didn't want to traumatize me, so it didn't give me any information on what happened to my parents. (Later, after a couple of session swabs, practitioners do session swabs, my SC told me that my parents abandoned me in the mine to die.) This explained the tremendous heartache in the mine. When Tracie directed me to where I lived, I entered the nicest house in a village with dirt roads. While everyone else lived in huts, I lived in a bungalow with an elderly lady. I learned that she was my grandma, and my parents owned that mine. She was my guardian and caretaker. Her love was so strong, and she guided me for that lifetime. She was my soulmate, and life with her was so good. Going forward in a future scene in that same life, I was in my teens. Sitting next to my grandma in an important seat, watching a parade and people dancing for us. I was in a beautiful dress and shoes. I felt confident and happy; I didn't have that heavy feeling in my heart anymore. There were lots of flowers everywhere. Tracie then moved me forward to an important day, where I was watching my little girl laughing. A tiny little vivacious girl with yellow ribbons in her ponytails. I wasn't married, it was just me and my cutest baby girl. It was the happiest time in that lifetime for me. Then I saw my grandma die, and since nobody else there loved me, I left the village with my baby girl. I raised my baby girl in the woods, a simple life to be a simple independent girl. We then moved forward to the last day of my life, immobilized on my bed with my daughter crying next to me. We had a great life together, but I was content to leave. My SC wanted to show me this past life to remind me that I have been a strong woman, and I have the strength to endure any situation thrown at me in this lifetime. There is no perfect. I came from money, and I left money to follow my heart and pursue a simpler life. After this, something strange happened during the session. I left that life behind and went into the dark.

It was a nice comfortable dark place, and I was resting. I didn't want to go anywhere else—that life was painful and I needed the rest. Tracie then moved me on. Next thing I knew, I was thrust into the light. I had to sit in this white light. This white light was powerful, and almost overbearing, but all I felt was love. A strange feeling came over me, like I've been here before, and it felt like a kind of love that I have never felt before. Perhaps this is what unconditional love feels like! I loved receiving and bathing in this light, but then I was being told I have to go somewhere again. I was reluctant because it was so nice to be there in the light. I could bathe in this light forever!

That was the portion of a past life I experienced. I didn't find it traumatizing, but I was surprised at the reason why the SC showed me that life. It reminded me that I can be remarkable and simple. Apparently, I have had a difficult time figuring that out in this lifetime. My SC said, Life is worth the love and simplicity. Money isn't important. She had the money and ran away from it and still lived a remarkably happy life. My SC continued to explain how I ended up with my contracts in this life.

"She was raised by a strong feminine figure, raised her daughter by herself, and didn't feel the masculinity in that life; therefore, she wanted to feel the masculinity in this life. This is why everyone in her house—even her cat—are males, and she worked in an industry filled with men. When she chose this life, she wanted to surround herself with male energy because she didn't experience it in that previous life. She also wanted to know what aggression feels like, and she has had a good dose of it in this lifetime. Men invigorate her with their amazing ideas and their ability to grow, perform, and make things come true, which is fascinating to her. Male energies are more complicated, while female energies are easier to work with. Because of this, she wants to be a female for the rest of her lives on earth."

That was a strange response. Never in my life would I have consciously said these words. However, my SC gave a good answer to my original question of why are there so many male figures in my life.

BEAR

When Tracie asked about Bear, my SC said that Bear chose me to be his mom because I could handle the intricacies of his medical condition. Bear specifically came in to learn as quickly as possible, and he's looking for his special person because she is going to help him get well. Spiritually, in his undeveloped state, the breakdown was from an inability to understand life and his purpose at that young age. His spiritual awakening was rough, but it was his journey to take as he finds his path in life. Tracie surrogate healed Bear through me by revealing that the hormones and chemistry of his body was off due to puberty. This would take time to adjust, and it was a lesson for me to learn how to let go. I didn't need to push the medications or the therapist, I just needed to let him go fly and be free to find his soulmate.

MARRIAGE

On my marriage, my SC reminded me that Dean loves me more than I know. I was going through a hate phase where nothing pleased me.

"She's a hard person. Hard on herself and hard on everyone around her. But she needs to know it's going to be difficult to find anyone to put up with her. For that, she should stay in the marriage. She needs to let go of controlling her marriage, and it will make her happier."

Tracie then asked, "Why is she hard on herself?" My SC replied

"She just wants the best for herself and her loved ones. As a female growing up, she learned that you had to be the best, academically and financially, to live a remarkable life. It's important that she shows this."

Learning this from my SC was a hard pill to swallow. Now that I have achieved academic and financial success, I have no reason to be hard on myself nor anyone around me anymore.

BUSINESS

Regarding my business, my SC said,
"That's her baby, too. She came into this life to build something big and to help people. She has built a community that teaches people how to manufacture food and feed themselves.

When they learn how to feed themselves, it will alleviate the suffering around the world. She has to collaborate with the right people who care. She has already served her purpose there."

HEALTH

In terms of my health, my SC didn't slow down.

"The ring on her finger cannot come off because her fingers are swollen. This is from her hormones from the right organ (my liver). Being premenopausal, she is hormonally imbalanced; therefore, she's mad all of the time. She needs to stop being mad at people that have been mean or prejudiced toward her. Stop being mad at the world for things that she cannot change. She can try Reiki to adjust her energy, or just stop being mad."

Tracie asked, "How about the weight?" My SC said

"She's holding too much inside of her, and she needs to let go. She is scared if she's not in control because she doesn't know what life would look like. She has always been in control!"

Tracie asked," What does it look like to her if she's not in control?" My SC replied,

"To not do a gazillion things at a time. Not worry about the mess. Just lie down, and not get up. Just lie in bed. Don't worry about the boys. Don't worry about the husband. Sit in the light and meditate. She needs to let go of the anger and the control —to not blame her parents and her brother for anything and just love them for who they are. They are who they are. Their actions are not hers to carry. Let it go."

Tracie asked, "Is there anything in her diet that she can fix to help the hormones?" My SC said,

"Eggs, more eggs. She doesn't eat them enough."

Tracie asked, "how about her fatty liver? She said she

healed it, so how can she prevent it from returning?" My SC said,

"Her liver needs love. She doesn't love herself. It's the anger hormones—she needs to let go. Once she releases the anger, she will find love for herself, and her liver will be fine. Exercise and muscles help release anger. Alcohol, too."

Tracie wrestled with my SC on recommending alcohol: "You're not creating a raging alcoholic, are you?" My SC replied,

"Alcohol would be the fastest way for her to relax and release the anger. Maybe one or two drinks a week. But don't worry, she won't be an alcoholic because she doesn't like the taste."

"How about her high blood sugar," Tracie continued. My SC replied,

"She loves sugar. She probably will get diabetes."

Tracie then rebutted, "You are her SC, and you can adjust. You can do anything, can't you?" To which my SC responded,

"Sugar makes her happy. She's not happy right now, and the anger makes it worse."

Tracie then suggested, "if she released her anger, it would help her with her blood sugar, too?" My SC replied,

"Yes. If she pursues her dreams of being a practitioner, she would not be so angry and wouldn't need the sugar as much."

Tracie then asked a new question: "How about her Cholesterol? Why is it high?" My SC responded,

"Anger also. Anger is kept in her liver, reducing the function of her liver; therefore, the processing of cholesterol is not good."

So as you can see, I have anger issues. If I worked on my anger, a majority of my health issues would go away. While this sounds simple and straightforward, the process of letting go of anger, and letting go of control, is a multi-layered process. I had so much work to do!

ANGER

The next part of the hypnosis was comical as Tracie wrestled with my SC to release the anger.

Tracie, "If anger were a shape, what would it be? Inside or outside of the body?"

My SC, "A BIG red sphere, front right center in front of me. It grows, but I'm afraid to pop it, in case it splatters everywhere like when you pop a big zit!"

Tracie, "What if it doesn't create a mess?"

My SC, "Hmmmmm."

Tracie, "Can she change the size of it?? Can she do that?"

My SC, "Yes, by not giving it too much power."

Tracie, "What happens if she doesn't give it too much power?"

My SC, "The ball is now small."

Tracie, " Can everything heal now?

My SC, "Yes, everything can heal. Everything is going to be fine."

Before bringing me out of hypnosis, Tracie asked my SC one last time if there are any messages for me.

My SC responded,

"Stay safe and do not go out alone in the wilderness. She needs to go with her husband. She needs to bring him with her. She's been too independent. She needs to go camping with the trailer, be next to the ocean, and sight-see with him. She would love it with him."

Foraging for wild mushrooms in the Pacific Northwest is popular, and in recent years, illegal commercial picking has increased on public land. I believe these pickers had everything to do with an expert forager going missing. She probably came across their buckets and told them off. This is why my SC cautioned me not to go picking by myself.

"One more thing, she will have lots of grandchildren, and she's not happy about that. Too many people to worry about."

Tracie then replied, "Will the children be fine?" My SC said,

"They won't be how she would like them to be. Totally independent little beings like her. She just needs to say "That's okay." This should be her new mantra." "That's okay, I love me."

21

THE DO-OVER

"Healing doesn't mean the damage never existed. It means the damage no longer controls your life."
   -Akshay Dubey

C oming out of the trance felt like a hangover of some sort. It didn't feel real, and my body struggled to get back into this reality. Because this was my first time, I literally had to find my feet and my footing as I got off the bed. I vividly remembered all that was said in that session, or so I thought. The summary session after the hypnosis was a quick wrap up and a reminder from Tracie to listen to my recording, as the healing would continue from there.

I was back to my normal life again. I didn't see any big changes. All of the things we talked about changed my mood, but it didn't change me physically. One day, about two weeks after the session, I was going for a run on the Oregon coast, my favorite place to be. I decided to finally listen to Tracie's session, and every time I listened to it, I cried at my past life segment. I wasn't sad about it, tears just flowed out. I guess my soul connected deeply to that past life. I thought I remembered everything that happened in the hypnosis, but there were parts of it that I didn't even remember saying! I listened to it three times (like my SC told me to), and I listened to it consecutively on three days while running.

On the fourth day, all of a sudden, I realized I didn't need my reading glasses anymore. That's strange, I didn't ask for healing on my eyes, so how could this happen? In the next few weeks, I slept better, and in the next few months, I completely got my sleep back. I didn't ask for healing there either. I believed that the listening of the recording helped me continue to release the anger and the need to control everything. This eventually reduced my need for sugar, reducing my blood sugar, and improving my eyesight. My liver cleared up, too, due to my release of the anger. With that, my moods were better, my hormones changed, and I could go back to getting seven to eight hours of sleep at night. The improvement in my sleep helped with the hormones, which put me in better moods. This eventually helped me let go of a lot, including blocks in my life. The removal of these blocks also eradicated my allergy to cat/dogs and detergents. I'm no longer allergic to these things anymore. With guidance from my SC on my business, I released the stress from that area of my life, and it resulted in the eradication of my bruxism. I no longer need a mouth guard when I sleep at night. This was how hypnosis changed my life. It gave back my health with step-by-step instructions on how to take care of the problems. I was sold. I was going to pay for the online courses so I could heal Bear! But, oh wow. I was in for a wild ride.

I thought I was going to get a how-to handbook and slides, but it was watching hours after hours of Dolores teaching her unique method of hypnosis. Not only could I not stop watching, but I felt incredibly blessed that I witnessed the Master speak her craft. I adore that woman, and every word she spoke stuck in my mind. I mean, after all, she is a hypnotist!

In order to get certified and practice, practitioners need to do an internship of hypnotizing 25 people without charging them. So, the journey started, and I stumbled so badly.

I successfully hypnotized my first friend using Dolores's procedure. It was easy. Then the next 10 friends were bumpy. Some couldn't get hypnotized, and some even slept! You see, getting them into Theta was easy, keeping them there required practice! However, I kept going, and the more friends I hypnotized, the better I got. I want to thank all of my friends who volunteered for this. You have really helped me hone this craft to heal Bear, and you are always welcomed back to my practice!

There is an incredible community and resource in the program's community forum. It was where I went when I had questions, and I had lots of questions. That's where I met all of the Masters of this craft. Not only were they at the highest levels of QHHT®, they are also so full of love and support, and they have always had time for us novices. Sometimes I feel so lucky to have chanced upon this program. To this day, their words still inspire me to move on and keep practicing, regardless of the hurdles. There is a secret in the community called session swaps. This is where interns and practitioners swap sessions. It's the easiest way to get practice in while getting feedback on your technique. I wasn't expecting this, but every swap I did, my SC got in deeper. With every session, I was able to get answers for this life and my healing continued on. It also opened up my channel, my connection to Source. It was because of the five session swaps that I have now done a 180 degree with my life. My mission in life has changed, and all of my health problems have disappeared. One friend from Finland even commented that I have completely changed from a few years back when she last saw me. "I like you better now than before," said Inna. You cannot beat that Finnish honesty!

◎ What Is Source Energy?

Source energy is not some floaty, new-age concept reserved for people who eat kale and wear crystals in their bras.

Source is the realest thing there is.

It's the thing behind the thing.

The force behind the breath.

The hum beneath everything that exists.

You can call it God, the Universe, the Divine, the Quantum Field, Higher Self, Spirit, or "that feeling you get when you're alone in nature and everything suddenly makes sense." It doesn't care what you name it. It just is.

Source is unconditional love. It doesn't punish. It doesn't abandon. It doesn't get moody or withhold your blessings because you forgot to meditate this week.

It's infinite, intelligent, creative energy and it's what you're made of.

You don't "connect" to Source.

You are Source.

You just forget. And that's okay. Because part of being human is learning to remember.

When you're in alignment with Source, things flow. Not because life gets easier, but because you stop fighting yourself. You stop chasing validation, and start choosing resonance. You stop begging for love, and start becoming the kind of love that heals everything it touches.

This isn't about becoming something new.

It's about stripping away everything you were never meant to carry.

So the part of you that's eternal, magnetic, and wildly powerful can finally breathe again.

Something happened to me on my second session swap. All of a sudden, I had these downloads come into my meditation. The white light that I usually focused on during my meditations also became stronger, and I felt the same love that I had felt when Tracie was bringing me out of the past life. Could this be true? Can I now access Source energy? Well, let me try. When I started writing the guided meditations, the downloads came and words just flowed right through me. These are images and words that I have not worked with before in all of my science writing, and it came so easily. I would like to call it my channel to Source energy. Now, during meditation I am able to connect clearly with Source energy, and we communicate all of the time. Source energy informed me that I have to make my work and my meditations as easily accessible as possible because there are too many people suffering right now who need access to this relief. Source said to me that they didn't guide me to build my digital resource for nothing, and I needed to utilize my skills that were learned there to build out the same media for my practice. I started publishing my work. You can find me on Soundcloud under Lotus White Light, and on the Free Insight Timer App under Lotus Cheong.

One of the session swaps also showed me the network of practitioners and our job in guiding people to the New Earth. The same New Earth that Eckert Tolle published about. Source energy mentioned that I was to collaborate and partner with many people and organizations to elevate the consciousness and vibrations of people so they can enter the New Earth, and this is partly why I published this book. I am calling out to my Soul sisters and brothers, all energy healers and light workers, to join me in building this community to transcend to the New Earth. This is not a physical transcendence, but a spiritual and emotional one. Please join me on the Facebook page called 5D Coalition. We will connect and build the grid from there.

It almost felt comical how I had spent so much energy building up to that one session, only to return to laundry, deadlines, and dishes. The everyday had returned in full force, but I wasn't quite the same person navigating it. I was slower somehow, not in movement, but in how I took in the world around me. I watched more. I observed more. I was more attuned to the subtle energetic ripples that had once been background noise. Now, they were foreground symphonies.

Listening to the recording while running helped me experience the session differently each time. New meanings would jump out at me. The emotions didn't dull if anything, they became more nuanced. I could feel the layers of grief, power, joy, confusion, and love that flowed through my subconscious. It was like watching a film of my soul. Sometimes, I stopped running altogether, tears streaking down my cheeks, grateful there were no strangers around to see.

In the days that followed, I noticed subtle shifts. I became more patient with Bear. Instead of jumping to solutions or treatments, I listened. Really listened. He seemed calmer. Maybe it was a coincidence. Maybe not. Tracie had said healing would continue long after the session, especially as I integrated what was revealed.

From there, small things changed. I started allowing myself to leave projects half finished. I stopped micromanaging. I let the boys be loud without always shushing them. I let myself rest not collapse-from-burnout rest, but intentional, soul-nourishing stillness. I started to taste what surrender could feel like.

It was intoxicating.

Tracie had told me during the session that integration would be the real work. She wasn't kidding. One afternoon, Bear was having a tough moment. His energy was frantic and scattered, and he was unable to self-regulate. Instead of jumping in with directions or corrections, I sat beside him and asked, "What do you need from me right now?" He looked at me, stunned. I could tell no one had asked him that before.

He blinked and said, "I don't know."

"That's okay," I replied. "We'll figure it out together."

That moment changed everything. It was the beginning of

a new chapter in our relationship, one grounded in trust instead of urgency.

My relationship with Dean began to soften too. There was a day I came home from the store, saw him mopping the floor, and instead of pointing out the missed spots like I usually did, I just said, "Thank you for doing that." He looked at me like I had grown another head. I realized that affirmation had been in short supply, and I had been the gatekeeper of so much of it in our home.

We didn't change overnight, but the small gestures added up. Laughter returned more often. Arguments de-escalated faster. I noticed myself choosing grace over sarcasm, curiosity instead of judgment.

Meanwhile, I was also paying attention to the foods I ate. I started incorporating more eggs, like my SC suggested. It wasn't just about nutrition, it felt symbolic. A gesture of listening to myself. I even bought whiskeys, remembering the SC's advice about softening. Now. If only I can get over that terrible taste of hard liquor....

Life continued, but I began to meet it differently. Not with fists up, but with hands open.

By the end of that season, I understood what the session had gifted me: not just information, but transformation. Not just insight, but permission. Permission to be softer. Permission to not have it all figured out. Permission to love without guarding. Most importantly, permission to love myself, even in the mess.

This was the do-over I never knew I needed.

This was my ride. My ride back to myself.

22

THE FREQUENCY OF FREEDOM

"As you shift your frequency, your reality begins to shift with you."
-Abraham Hicks

"My life has practically turned around, and I don't even recognize myself anymore," said one of my very first clients. That's exactly how I feel too, now that I've been given this do-over. It wasn't just for me. If this kind of transformation was possible for me, and for her, then it could be possible for others. That realization became the foundation of my hypnosis practice. "You've shown me there is no barrier to entry when it comes to connecting with Source and experiencing this level of healing," Inna said after her session. That's when I knew. I wasn't just guiding people into deep states of consciousness: I was helping them access their own power. This was the essence of why I became a healer, why I chose to be a practitioner.

As I gave more sessions, I learned. And with each new soul that came to me, I grew some more. I started to notice a shift in the kinds of questions people were asking. A change in the energy they carried. There was a resonance, a deep pull, toward something more expansive, more heart-centered. Something we now call the 5D life.

So what is 5D?

The Fifth Dimensional world is a spiritual term. We're currently living in a Three dimensional (3D) world. It's the world most of us were born into. A world governed by physical laws like time, space, gravity, and logic. In 3D, things are very black and white. Good or bad. Right or wrong. Masculine or feminine. It's a world of duality, of constant comparison, and of needing to prove ourselves to survive.

The Fourth Dimension (4D) adds something different. In 4D, we begin to become aware of ourselves as more than just physical bodies. We start to tap into energy and emotion. Meditation, mindfulness, lucid dreaming these are all doorways into the 4D realm. It's a necessary bridge, but it's still transitional. It's where the inner work begins, where we begin to witness our thoughts and peel back layers.

And then there's the Fifth Dimension (5D). This is the realm beyond the illusion of separation. It's where unity consciousness resides, and time unfolds more like a spiral than a straight line., It's where unconditional love isn't earned, it simply is. In 5D, there's no need to hustle for your worth. You don't need to be fixed, saved, or validated. You just are. Whole. Complete. Interconnected with everyone and everything. Living in 5D means leading from your heart, choosing from love, trusting your inner knowing, and flowing with life instead of against it.

This isn't some abstract spiritual theory. I've seen this shift happen in real people, my client above being one of them. I watched it bloom in Inna. And in so many of my clients who walk in carrying anxiety, shame, or grief and walk out lighter, clearer, softer. More themselves. After connecting with their higher selves through hypnosis, their energy shifts. Their choices, their relationships, even the rhythm of their breath everything begins to vibrate on a new frequency.

In one session, a woman sobbed over a heartbreak that happened twenty years ago. When her SC came through, it said: "She never healed because she believed she didn't deserve love. But she does. She always has." Just that one message caused her body to relax. She left saying she felt twenty pounds lighter. That's not a metaphor. That's 5D energy work in action. You start moving into the New Earth.

The New Earth isn't a place it's a frequency. It's a way of living where love leads, truth heals, and every soul remembers its power. This New Earth we're moving into, this collective vibration of 5D living, isn't reserved for spiritual leaders or monks on mountaintops. It's accessible to everyone. The woman who is exhausted from trying to do it all. The man who has been told his emotions are a weakness. The child who feels like they don't belong. This is an invitation to all of us.

You begin the shift by choosing love. Over and over again. Even when it's hard. Especially when it's hard. You soften instead of harden. You allow instead of resist. You become the observer instead of the reactor. That's when the magic begins. But it's not magic, it's resonance. It's a vibration. It's science.

Let me explain.

In physics, there's something called entrainment. When two objects with different vibrations are placed near each other, the one with the stronger, steadier frequency pulls the other into sync. This happens with pendulum clocks. Tuning forks. Heartbeats. Even brainwaves.

So when you choose love instead of fear, your entire system starts vibrating differently. That frequency of calm, open, grounded, starts radiating outward. And it starts pulling everything else into harmony with it. Your thoughts. Your body. Your relationships. Your environment.

You're not "manifesting."

You're becoming a vibrational match to the life that already exists at that frequency.

That's the resonance.

That's alignment.

That's how Source energy works. Through physics, not fairy dust.

My own life has become a walking case study of what happens when you align with this frequency. I have learned that living in 5D doesn't mean you never get angry or sad. It means you no longer identify with those emotions. You feel them, honor them, and then you release them. You don't hoard pain anymore. You let it move through you like wind through trees.

Now, with my own practice, clients often ask me, "How do I get there?" I tell them: "You're not going anywhere." The New Earth isn't a place. It's a frequency you tap into. Your body knows how to get there when you practice 5D living, especially after a hypnosis session. It remembers. Every time you choose forgiveness, every time you trust, every time you let go you get closer.

Getting to your SC is where you remember who you are. 5D Living will keep you there vibrating at the New Earth frequency.

And that is what this chapter, and this work, is all about.

23

BACK TO LOVE

"Your task is not to seek for love, but merely to seek and find all the barriers within yourself that you have built against it."
   -Rumi

This book isn't about divorcing my husband. That much is clear now. The real divorce the one that unraveled me and then stitched me back together, was from a life that no longer fit. A life that now feels like someone else's entirely. A version of me I can barely remember, but whose pain I wore like skin.

That life was built on structure, ambition, control, and fear. It was always about doing more, performing better, and outpacing failure. I was driven, accomplished, and admired; but I was also slowly and invisibly crumbling on the inside. I had checked all the boxes, fulfilled all of the cultural and familial expectations, I was being good, but I still felt unaccomplished.

At first, I thought I was leaving Dean. I was convinced our marriage was the root of my dissatisfaction. I couldn't breathe within our routines. I blamed him for not changing, not grow-ing, and not seeing me. But what I didn't realize at the time was that I wasn't seeing myself, either. Dean didn't trap me. I had built the trap with my own two hands, from a blueprint handed to me by generations of women before me.

When I stepped into that first hypnosis session, I wasn't expecting the ground to shift beneath me. I was looking for answers about Bear. But what I found was something so much deeper. I found myself.

Bear's journey had broken me wide open. His health struggles, his resistance, his sensitivity, his anger they were mirrors. Every flare-up and shutdown moved something within me I hadn't faced. I thought I needed to fix him. Instead, I learned how to stop trying to fix everything. I learned to let go.

Through hypnosis, I discovered that our children choose us. They arrive with their own wisdom and contracts. Bear chose me because I could walk beside him on a path few others would understand. He came here to learn quickly, to struggle early, and to evolve beyond the noise. While I had been trying to pull him out of the storm, the real work was to stand in my own center and let him find his way. He didn't need saving. I did.

And I found it.

Hypnosis didn't just introduce me to my subconscious, it reintroduced me to my soul. My Theta sessions took me back to lives where I had loved, lost, sacrificed, and stood strong. I reconnected with the core of who I have always been: a researcher, a teacher, and a healer. But I had buried my true self under layers of productivity and performance.

Each chapter of this book told a piece of that story. Chapter one began with my unraveling, feeling like a stranger in my own body and life. Chapter by chapter, I confronted the cultural programming that shaped me, the loneliness of motherhood, the guilt of being "too much" and "not enough," and the way I had allowed success to define my self-worth.

I faced the emotional weight of being the perfect daughter, the good wife, and the successful entrepreneur. I traced the internalized expectations back to their roots. My upbringing, my family's sacrifices, the quiet trauma of assimilation. I held a magnifying glass to the dissonance between my professional accolades and my emotional exhaustion.

Chapter 20 was a turning point in my life! My session with Tracie opened the door to the Theta realm, and what awaited me there was breathtaking. Floating weightless, surrounded by light, I accessed a part of me that I never knew existed. A part that was always whole. It reminded me that simplicity was strength. That love was the only real currency. That I didn't have to prove my worth. I just had to remember it.

I didn't just meet my higher self. I became them.

Then came the integration. The hard part. The part where you return to your waking life with new eyes and realize nothing fits the same way anymore. Food tastes different. Conversations hit differently. Silence becomes a teacher. Your body wants to move more slowly, speak more softly, and love more deeply.

I left behind an old identity, the "woman who does it all." The hustler. The fixer. The lady boss. I realized that many of those labels had been armor, not achievements.

So what took its place?

Creativity. Peace. Connection. Laughter. Service.

I began making art again, cutting rocks, polishing gemstones, learning to wire wrap and cast silver. I started teaching others in the Past Lives studio, giving second chances, not just to materials, but to people. I started playing music. My steel tongue drum became my meditation. I recorded guided visualizations, uploaded them to Insight Timer, and watched people find peace through my voice. It blew my mind.

My marriage softened, too. Dean and I didn't split. Instead, I let go of the version of him I had been trying to force into existence. I stopped pushing for change and started appreciating what was. And somehow, through the grace of it all, love returned. Not as a grand gesture, but in quiet mornings, shared jokes, and mutual respect. We were able to grow together this time, without resentment.

This book is not about ending a marriage. It's about ending a performance. It's about awakening to the soul beneath the roles.

It's about returning.

Returning to your body. To your intuition. To your joy. To the sacredness of being alive.

To love.

I live differently now. I eat when I'm hungry. I rest without apology. I am softer. I say "no" with grace. I laugh with my son on the phone. I kiss my husband goodnight. I cry during meditation. I forgive people who never said sorry.

And I keep going.

Not to prove anything, but because I've come home to myself.

This is what a spiritual awakening really looks like. Not walking away from your life, but finally stepping fully into it. Raw. Honest. Unfiltered.

The shift wasn't just energetic. It was cellular. It was the journey from survival to sovereignty. From performing to presence. From being a good wife to being my whole self.

If you're wondering what's next for me, I don't have the answer. But I can tell you this.

I'm not going back.

Exit the Good Wife is not just a title. It's a permission slip. To leave the story you were handed. To stop performing for love. To remember who you were before the world told you who to be.

This book began with a woman who was exhausted from pretending.

It ends with a woman who is finally free.

And that, my friend, is the miracle.

The exit is where it all begins.

ACKNOWLEDGMENTS

This book would not exist without the layered beauty, pain, and transformation that life has gifted me, nor without the people who walked beside me, sometimes gently, sometimes painfully, as I found my voice again.

To my husband, Dean. Thank you for staying, for enduring, for allowing the slow unraveling of my many selves as I learned to see you more clearly, and to love you from a truer place.

To my children, you have been my greatest teachers. Your courage to walk through darkness and your willingness to be fully seen have changed me at my core. You gave this story its reason. Thank you for choosing me to be in your contracts.

To all my reviewers, Melody Rowell, Liz Lemkey, Sunita Sukumaran and Elizabeth Chua. I'm so grateful for your time. The honesty in your feedback provided the clarity I needed to get this book ready for publication.

To Mark Grimes, the Godfather of Portland Startups and marketing genius, whose visionary spirit, relentless curiosity, awkward frankness, and unwavering belief in community lit the spark for so many of us to begin. You are truly an ally for women, and I'm grateful for your support for my entrepreneurial journey.

To Dominique Low, Masie Ong, Bernice Tan, Sunita Sukumaran, Choo Wei Tan, Siew Ling Wong and Angela Ho. Thank you for helping me pick up pieces of myself when I couldn't.

To Tracie Mahan, your guidance through the Theta realm

opened a door that will never close. Thank you for holding space with grace and strength while I met the pieces of myself I thought were long buried.

To my first 25 clients, your support meant so much to me. Your willingness to open your heart and let me test this procedure on you truly showed me how much you cared for Bear and me. I am eternally grateful that you helped me begin the journey toward the life my soul came here to live.

To my clients, you may not know this, but each session with you gave me the permission to be honest with myself. I am honored that you shared your journey with me. You taught me that healing is a communal act.

To Dolores Cannon, your legacy continues. Your technique went through decades of fine tuning, and it is perfect the way it is. Thank you for the method that opened my heart and cracked my soul wide open to live in the 5D world, and for creating a tight-knit and loving community. I can't thank you enough and all my QHHT® sisters and Julia Cannon, for the support on this journey.

To my parents and my brother, who have given me their all while enduring their own hardships. I understand your suffering and I do not blame you at all. I did well with my contract.

Thank you to Steve Edwards, Brian Gerath and Sampathkumar J., for your work in producing this book.

To my ancestors and guides, thank you for whispering through the veil and showing me that I am never alone.

And finally, to the version of me who was brave enough to start this journey, to sit in front of a blank page, and to write not just from truth, but from the trembling, pulsing ache of love. I see you. I thank you. I love you unconditionally.

ABOUT THE AUTHOR

Lotus Cheong is not your average memoirist. She's a scientist-turned-soul-seeker, entrepreneur, mother, QHHT® practitioner, and unapologetic truth-teller. After years of doing everything "right" like building a business, raising a family, being the good wife—she blew the lid off her carefully curated life and began telling the truth. First to herself, then to everyone else.

Through her own healing odyssey, Lotus discovered the radical power of past life regression, subconscious guidance, and the sacred art of saying, "No more." Her work is rooted in 5D consciousness, emotional liberation, and the audacity to laugh through the mess. Her mission is bigger than just words on a page. It's a full-body permission slip for women everywhere to exit the lives they've outgrown.

When she's not writing or guiding clients through quantum journeys, you'll find her rockhounding, foraging, or making jewelry from the stones she digs up. Literal reminders that transformation is hidden in the dirt and mess. Lotus now leads soul-shaking retreats, where individuals gather to remember who they are beneath the roles they've been performing. You can view her work, and join her retreats at LotusCheong.com

This is her first book. But let's be clear: it's not just a book. It's a portal, a permission slip, and an incantation for every woman ready to exit the script and reclaim the story her soul came here to tell.